THE DISCERNING HEART

Exploring the Christian Path

Wilkie W. Au
and
Noreen Cannon Au

PAULIST PRESS
New York/Mahwah, N.J.

A number of the quotations that appear in this book were written before the current sensitivity to inclusive language was an issue. The reader is asked to read the quotations in the inclusive manner in which they were intended, even when the language used is exclusive to modern eyes.

Cover design by Joy Taylor

Library of Congress Cataloging-in-Publication Data

Au, Wilkie, 1944-
The discerning heart : exploring the Christian path /
Wilkie W. Au and Noreen Cannon Au.
p. cm.
Includes index.
ISBN 0-8091-4372-0 (alk. paper)
1. Discernment (Christian theology) 2. Decision making—Religious aspects—Christianity. 3. Decision making—Psychological aspects. 4. Providence and government of God. I. Au, Noreen Cannon, 1945- II. Title.
BV4509.5A88 2006
248.4'82—dc22
2005025496

Published by Paulist Press
997 Macarthur Boulevard
Mahwah, New Jersey 07430

www.paulistpress.com

Printed and bound in the
United States of America

CONTENTS

In loving Memory
of our parents
James and Catherine Cannon
Tai Hing and Violet Au
whose
steadfast love
has inspired and strengthened
our
journey of faith

ACKNOWLEDGMENTS

The process of writing this book has evoked a deep sense of gratitude for what we each received from the thirty-two years we spent living in a religious community. The community was the caring context in which we learned theoretically and experientially what we share in this volume about discernment. As faith communities that are repositories of the accumulated wisdom of many saintly people, religious orders are able to hand on the richness of tradition. So we are glad to have this chance to acknowledge our indebtedness to the California Province of the Society of Jesus and the Los Angeles Province of the Sisters of St. Joseph of Carondelet.

We thank Sr. Mona Castelazo, CSJ, for her careful review of our manuscript and for her many perceptive and sensitive suggestions for improving the text. We are also grateful to Barbara Murphy and especially Deb Pavelek for their help with proofreading the final copy and preparing the index.

We thank in a special way our students, clients, and spiritual directees who have graciously given us permission to incorporate their personal stories into the book. Their experience provides concrete and vivid illustrations that are helpful for understanding the complex dimensions of the discernment process.

Finally, we thank our family, friends, and professional colleagues whose faithful encouragement and love support us in all of our endeavors.

W.W.A.
Loyola Marymount University
Los Angeles, California

N.C.A.
C.G. Jung Institute
Los Angeles, California

We are also grateful for permissions granted to use the following material:

Excerpts from Denise Levertov, *New & Selected Poems* (Bloodaxe Books, 2003). Used with permission.

Excerpts from Denise Levertov, from *Sands of the Well*, copyright © 1994, 1995, 1996 by Denise Levertov. Reprinted by permission of New Directions Publishing Corp.

Excerpts from "The Road Ahead" from *Thoughts in Solitude* by Thomas Merton. Copyright © 1958 by the Abbey of Our Lady of Gethsemani. Copyright renewed 1986 by the Trustees of the Thomas Merton Legacy Trust. Reprinted by permission of Farrar, Straus and Giroux, LLC.

Excerpts from *Letters to a Young Poet* by Rainer Maria Rilke (W. W. Norton & Company (1981).

Excerpts from "The Pulley of God," from *George Herbert: The Country Parson, the Temple,* ed. John N. Wall, Jr., copyright © 1981 by the Missionary Society of St. Paul the Apostle in the State of New York. Used with permission of Paulist Press: www.paulistpresss.com.

Introduction

DISCERNMENT AND CHRISTIAN GROWTH

TEN YEARS AGO WE BOTH WERE LIVING a very different life than we are today. Today we are "formers"—Wilkie, a former Jesuit priest, and Noreen, a former Sister of St. Joseph of Carondelet. How we arrived at where we are is a question we are frequently asked as people get to know us. Then, as they realize the answer is neither short nor simple, they invariably tell us, "You should write a book!" At first the more introverted one of us was uncomfortable with the curiosity and amazement our story evoked. The questions were hard to answer, and they seemed a bit too personal. As time passed, the more extroverted of us, who frequently lectures on spirituality and leads retreats and workshops, began to share his own journey of faith when speaking about prayer and discernment. To his surprise, he found that participants were not only receptive to his personal story but were strengthened and encouraged in their own faith journey.

Still, sharing one's experiences in the context of a talk and writing a book are two different things, and it would be another few years of living our story, now as a married couple, before it was integrated enough to give us the perspective from which to write. Now when people say, "You should write your story," we hear an underlying concern for some

1

shared wisdom about making important life choices as they or someone close to them face important crossroads or critical decisions. They recognize that some choices will be life altering, and they want to choose well. Down deep, what they really want to know is how to open themselves to the influence of God.

Our aim in writing this book is to address this spiritual question, a question that is at the heart of living as Christians. While not a book about "our story," we share what we have learned about making life choices in the context of living a life centered in God. We use personal examples occasionally when we think they flesh out a concept. We are aware that the particulars of each person's story are unique, but our journey of faith as Christian believers is in many ways the same. Interspersed too are insights and examples from our own clinical practice of over twenty-five years as a Jungian psychoanalyst (Noreen) and as a spiritual director (Wilkie). Respectful care has been taken at all times to honor the boundaries of professional confidentiality.

The focus of this book is attuning ourselves to the Spirit of God through the process called discernment. Our premise is straightforward: if God is the telling influence in our lives, this must be reflected in the way we make choices. We will focus on what it means to develop a discerning heart, a heart that seeks to be tuned in to the Spirit's guidance. Discernment takes on increased importance today because of several contemporary conditions: (1) increased longevity and the need to make important choices over the long haul; (2) the growing disillusionment with institutional authority; and (3) the developmental challenge of adult Christians to make decisions in a way that reflects their full stature as adults.

STAYING SPIRITUALLY ALIVE FOR THE LONG HAUL

To be alive is to face choices constantly. In the different seasons of our lives we are challenged to make choices that can best reconcile the innumerable desires we possess as human beings within a world of limits—some stemming from within our being and personality, others imposed from the outside world. Increased longevity makes lifelong discernment even more of a challenge. Human life expectancy in 1900 was forty-six years of age. In little more than one hundred years it has risen to seventy-nine. And the US Administration of Aging estimates that life expectancy at birth by 2050 will increase to eighty-six years for males and ninety-two years for females. Life choices are more complex today because, with increasing longevity and better health, we will be faced with more decisions than those living a generation ago.

In our middle years, for example, we will likely face the need to evaluate whether the career we are in is going to sustain us for the remainder of our working life. After twenty or twenty-five years certain dreams and goals have been fulfilled, and life becomes routine and predictable. Feelings of satisfaction and accomplishment may now be overshadowed by an unexplained restlessness that leads us to ask "What's wrong with me?" or "Is this all there is?" Such questions cannot be suppressed or devalued when retirement is still a long way off. A lurking danger at this point is what psychologists call entrapment or escalation of commitment. Entrapment "refers to the tendency to stick to prior decisions and attempt to justify them rather than having to admit mistakes and incur losses. The more one follows this course, the more one invests in the original decision and feels entrapped by it."[1] Whether we decide to continue on a certain path by reinvesting renewed energy or to make a significant change, what is important is that we identify our heart's desires and discern how we can best infuse vitality into the final portion of our work life. For some, the middle years also bring concerns and responsibility for aging parents: "Is it time to think about a nursing home for Dad?" "Mom is showing signs of Alzheimer's. What should we do?" "I have durable power of attorney. How do I know when to end Grandpa's life-support?" And in our post-retirement years we are once again faced with questions of meaning and purpose and must decide how we will spend our final years. Longevity brings with it decisions about health care, relationships, and time.

In these and other important questions of life, believers want to follow God's lead and make prayerful choices. But how are the movements of the Spirit to be detected? Where is God's guiding voice to be heard? The Book of Deuteronomy clearly points out the direction.

> Surely, this commandment that I am commanding you today is not too hard for you, nor is it too far away. It is not in heaven, that you should say, "Who will go up to heaven for us, and get it for us so that we may hear it and observe it?" Neither is it beyond the sea, that you should say, "Who will cross to the other side of the sea for us, and get it for us so that we may hear it and observe it?" No, the word is very near to you; it is in your mouth and in your heart for you to observe. (Deut 30:11–14)

A HOLISTIC APPROACH

Echoing Deuteronomy, this book on spiritual discernment emphasizes that the God whose guidance we seek is not distant but is in our midst. It is our job to become sensitive to the promptings of this God, who is everywhere to be found, in all the aspects of our lives. A holistic approach to discernment advocates a broad and wide-ranging search for divine guidance. It reflects the fact that "the impulse of contemporary times, and a positive sign in personal discernment, is toward widening the circle of dialogue, attentiveness, and affection."[2] Holistic discernment requires paying close attention to what goes on both in the external world and in our inner world of feelings and desires, thoughts and bodily sensations, dreams and fantasies, aspirations and fears. Taking seriously our own inner life as an important source of God's guidance can be a particular challenge for people. Many of us have been conditioned to distrust our personal experiences and intuitions and to look for "the truth," "the right answer," and "God's will" in outside authority. This prejudice against the inner workings of the Spirit leads easily to an unhealthy betrayal of the self, the intimate dwelling place of God. That is why Henri Nouwen encourages us to pay close attention to what is going on in our lives. "By slowly converting our loneliness into a deep solitude, we create that precious space where we can discover the voice telling us about our inner necessity—that is, our vocation."[3]

Spiritually attuned seekers can experience God's lead in multiple ways, as did the three magi who found God: in the very desire that launched their search for the Promised One; in their companionship and shared wisdom along the way; in a star that kept them on track; in the face of a newborn child lying in a manger; and in a dream that warned them not to return home by way of Herod's territory (Matt 2:1–12). Like the magi, contemporary Christians are increasingly embracing an image of God who is present in every nook and cranny of creation. The whole world is the vocabulary of God, and all reality can communicate divine guidance. Holistic discernment reflects this growing faith in a God of surprises who speaks through scripture, church teachings, other people, and external events, as well as in the silence of our hearts.

DISILLUSIONMENT WITH INSTITUTIONAL AUTHORITY

Whenever doubts about the credibility of recognized leaders weaken institutional authority, personal discernment takes on greater importance. Such was the case, for example, in the sixteenth century when the Roman Catholic Church was rife with corruption involving, among other things, the sale of benefices, which were ecclesiastical appointments under the control of bishops. This corrupt practice placed unfit leaders in charge of parishes and resulted in a scandalous neglect in pastoral care. Not only did such widespread corruption precipitate the Reformation, it also was the context for the rapid rise in influence of Saint Ignatius of Loyola, whose *Spiritual Exercises* ranks as one of the Christian classics on discernment.

In recent decades, corruption in government, business, and religious institutions have undermined confidence in institutional authority. In government, coverups have left Americans wondering how much they can trust their leaders. These scandals include the Watergate crisis in the 1970s, Irangate in the 1980s, the questioned outcome of the 2000 presidential election, recent doubts about how well the Federal Drug Administration (FDA) has functioned as an objective watchdog over the approval of new drugs, and persistent skepticism about the rationale for going to war in Iraq. In the business world the collapse of such firms as Enron and Arthur Andersen, the manipulation of gas and oil supplies, insider trading practices—to name only a few things—have eroded public trust in corporate America. And finally, sexual abuse by clergy has drastically shaken the confidence of believers in the reliability of their ordained leaders. Not surprisingly, this decline in institutional authority has been accompanied by the sober realization among lay Christians that they must assume greater responsibility for their lives, as well as for their church. While guarding against the danger of an exaggerated individualism, the historical circumstances in which we find ourselves today compel us to take much more responsibility than in the past for our decisions.

In the Roman Catholic Church, for example, the clergy sexual scandal has caused outraged Catholics to demand greater accountability from church officials and real participation in shaping ecclesial policies and structures. However, the underlying desire of a growing number of American Catholics is more basic; it is, simply, the cry to be treated as adults. Vatican II raised the hope that it is possible to be simultaneously adult and Catholic. But the movement toward an adult church has been thwarted by a hierarchy given to paternalism as well as by ultra-conservatives who prefer the "Father knows best" brand of religion. Together, these hierarchical and popular forces have often colluded in holding on to a model of childish dependence. Challenging the hierarchy to allow greater lay participation and autonomy is a two-edged sword; it simultaneously challenges lay Catholics to take more responsibility for the decisions that affect their lives and to acquire the skills needed for prayerful discernment.

Adult Decision-Making

Making choices as adult believers requires balancing two stances in creative tension. One stance is that of personal autonomy, which is our ability to stand on our own two feet as responsible and free individuals. The other stance is that of interdependence, which is our ability to acknowledge our need for others, not for security, but for help, support, and encouragement. The recognition of our interdependence as human beings does not diminish our autonomy but rather springs from it. Only when we have achieved a mature sense of identity and independence can we truly value and benefit from what others have to offer us. As believers in a God who is intimately involved in our lives, we are also challenged to integrate our total dependence on God's grace with the personal freedom and responsibility entrusted to us by our Creator.

The challenge is combining self-determination with a willingness to be led by the Spirit. Self-determination involves personally discovering our passions and desires and deciding how we will live them out in the world. Willingness to be led by the Spirit, as opposed to willfulness, opens us to the influence of others as we make these decisions. Self-determination and openness to the Spirit's guidance are not antithetical. Adult autonomy is achieved when we are willing to shape our lives through prayerful and responsible choices, not in isolation, but in dialogue with trusted others, aware that in the end the buck stops with us. If we have not achieved a healthy degree of autonomy, we will be either too compliant or too independent. We are too compliant when we conform passively to others' expectations and cave in to their dictates, as if we had no mind of our own. On the other hand, we are too independent when we automatically resist others' influence, as if they were infringing on our independence. Unsure that we can stand our ground, we close ourselves off completely to what they have to say.

FROM SUPEREGO TO SPIRIT

Adult Christian decision-making also entails making decisions that are increasingly based on conscious factors rather than on unconscious, internalized parental "shoulds" from childhood, what Freud called the "superego." These deeply ingrained prohibitions and demands are sometimes referred to as the voice of conscience. However, philosophers make an important distinction between the superego and conscience. The superego represents remnants of childhood training that guided our behavior prior to our acquiring the cognitive capacity to make proper choices on our own. Not meant to be a permanent mode of directing our choices, the superego is developmentally intended to be supplanted by conscience, which is our adult mind's ability to make independent judgments based on reflection.

As adult Christians we are called to make choices based on an informed conscience, which means deciding what is right or wrong based on sound information and reasoning. As a function of the practical intellect, conscience requires thoughtful deliberation, not an unreflective submission to the superego, which tells us what we need to do to maintain parental approval or to be a "good boy" or a "good girl." Furthermore, Christian spirituality challenges us to base our life choices not only on an informed conscience, but also on an inspired conscience. Inspiration speaks of the influence of God's Spirit. To have an inspired conscience is to allow the Spirit of God to permeate all aspects of our decision-making: our minds, our hearts, our bodies, our dreams, and our daydreams.

Personal autonomy does not come cheap; it requires the willingness to anguish through often complex and knotty issues. It calls for the willingness to suffer the discomfort of not having clear-cut answers and quick fixes. It calls for the patience and confidence to stay with conflicting inner and outer voices until we are able to sort out for ourselves what love asks of us and what the Spirit dictates. Fundamentalism, in all of its forms, undermines mature decision-making because it short-circuits personal deliberation. Prefabricated answers and solutions from some external source remove the need to struggle for our own truth—an essential struggle out of which an autonomous self can emerge.

Prone to black-and-white, either-or thinking, fundamentalism thwarts mature faith, which, according to James Fowler's stages of faith development, requires the embrace of paradox in the midst of complexity and mystery. Biblical fundamentalists, for example, narrowly confine God's voice and handicap their search for divine guidance. They straitjacket the truth by making "their literalist and simplistic interpretation [of scripture] the only legitimate one," states Episcopal Bishop J. Jon Bruno.[4] Others readily escape the anguish of personal search to rest in the security provided by unquestioning adherence to religious authority. Flight from personal responsibility is certainly understandable. We "may well shy away from some of its inevitable consequences: the increased level of anxiety it brings into our lives; the ambiguities of right and wrong, of good and better; the depth of commitment which a major decision entails. It seems as if personal freedom must be paid for by pain and suffering."[5]

Adult decision-making requires ongoing growth in the following directions:

- Movement away from facades, from a pretended self that we are not.
- Movement away from inner "shoulds" that originate from some idealized sense of what we must be to be acceptable, lovable, and worthwhile.

- Movement away from conformity for the sake of acceptance.
- Movement away from a compulsive need to please others that robs us of freedom.
- Movement toward greater openness to experience.
- Movement toward greater trust of self.
- Movement toward greater trust in God's ongoing faithfulness.
- Movement toward being self-directed and Spirit-led.

ADULT DISCIPLESHIP IN THE PATTERN OF JESUS

In Jesus, Christians have an ideal example of how to strike a healthy balance between being self-determined and Spirit-led. In accomplishing his God-given mission, Jesus clearly embodied both self-determination and fidelity to the Spirit. By following in his footsteps we can integrate autonomy and obedience, initiative and availability, creativity and receptivity.

The gospel clearly portrays Jesus as someone with a strong sense of personal autonomy. He possessed a sense of who he was and what he wanted to accomplish in life. His deeply rooted sense of identity and purpose allowed him to stay true to himself, even when he was misunderstood by his own family, deserted by his friends, and ridiculed by the religious establishment. Mark's Gospel recounts that his relatives "went out to restrain him, for people were saying, 'He has gone out of his mind'"(Mark 3:21). Moreover, John's Gospel relates that many of his disciples "turned back and no longer went about with him" (John 6:66), after hearing him proclaim that "unless you eat the flesh of the Son of Man and drink his blood, you have no life in you" (John 6:53). Near the end of his public ministry, Jesus' life was in danger and hence he "no longer walked about openly among the Jews" (John 11:54). Following the raising of Lazarus and all the excitement stirred up by that event, the chief priests and Pharisees decided that Jesus should be killed to maintain law and order and to reduce the risk of armed intervention by the Romans. Despite widespread opposition, Jesus pursued his mission with dogged determination. "When the days drew near for him to be taken up, he set his face to go to Jerusalem" (Luke 9:51). The phrase "set his face" is a Semitic expression used often in the Old Testament to connote opposition and hostility. Thus, setting his face toward the city where his mission would be fulfilled is a symbol of Jesus' single-minded determination.

That the Jesus portrayed by the Gospels was a self-possessed and autonomous person is unarguable. He stood his ground firmly and held on to his granite resolve to pursue his mission. He also had his own motives for pursuing his path, which was fraught with personal danger. Jesus made explicit that he was not a tragic hero whose life was being snatched from him by forces beyond his control. Rather, he asserted that "the Father loves me, because I lay down my life in order to take it up again. No one takes it from me, but I lay it down of my own accord. I have power to lay it down, and I have power to take it up again. I have received this command from my Father" (John 10:17–18). While Jesus exuded a strong sense of independence in all his actions, he never made personal autonomy an idol. His identity was grounded in an unswerving attachment to his Father's will. In this he demonstrated that being true to oneself is compatible with a deep willingness to follow God's desire. The supreme importance of obedience to God in the life of Jesus is illustrated throughout the Gospel of John. Consistently, Jesus links his personal identity to his filial relationship with God, whose work he was sent into the world to accomplish.

> "My food is to do the will of him who sent me and to complete his work." (John 4:34)

> "I can do nothing on my own. As I hear, I judge; and my judgment is just, because I seek to do not my own will but the will of him who sent me." (John 5:30)

> "When you have lifted up the Son of man, then you will know that I am he and that I do nothing of myself: what the Father has taught me is what I preach; he who sent me is with me, and has not left me to myself, for I always do what pleases him." (John 8:28–29)

> "I do as the Father has commanded me, so that the world may know that I love the Father." (John 14:31)

These texts leave no doubt that Jesus valued obedience to his Father as strongly as he cherished his personal autonomy. Even more important, they convey the truth that his relationship with God formed the basis of his self-understanding. Jesus cannot be understood without reference to the One who sent him. His central identity as Son linked him inextricably to God as Father. The same is true for us. Our primary identity as creatures links us inextricably to God as creator.

CHOOSING WITH GOD IS THE HEART OF ADULT OBEDIENCE

Authentic Christian obedience exists when we recognize God's influence upon our lives and when we experience ourselves finding God in what we do. Christian obedience acknowledges the fact that our relationship with God is as real and important as our relationship with our spouse, our close family members, and our friends. The opinions of people close to us make a difference in how we choose. What they think may not ultimately determine what we decide, but we nevertheless feel the need to consider what they say as part of our decision-making process. In other words, people who are central to our lives, unlike those to whom we are only peripherally connected, have a *telling* influence in our lives. In this sense obedience stems from our feeling that God is the most important relationship we have and reflects our desire to let God into the process when making major life choices. Our love for God makes God *the* telling influence in our life. Thus, obedience entails prayerfully listening to the voice of God in the many ways in which it is addressed to us and allowing God to influence our choices.

HOLISTIC DISCERNMENT AS A SPIRITUAL DISCIPLINE

Holistic discernment is a spiritual discipline that connects us with the Spirit and, as such, requires conscious and focused effort. As Jesus stated to Nicodemus, the senior Pharisee who sought guidance from Jesus in a nighttime rendezvous, the Spirit of God moves mysteriously like the wind, which "blows where it chooses, and you hear the sound of it, but you do not know where it comes from or where it goes" (John 3:8). We cannot create the wind of the Spirit; we cannot control the wind. All we can do is to set up the sail of our lives so that when the mysterious wind of the Spirit sweeps in, we can receive it and let our lives be powered by grace. Whatever we can do to position the sail of our lives in such a receptive way is part of the spiritual discipline we call holistic discernment.

A zen story recounts the experience of a young Japanese worker who was disillusioned with his worldly pursuits and weary from overwork. Leaving behind the clamoring metropolis of Tokyo, he went to Eiheiji, the Buddhist monastery serenely situated in the beautiful Japanese Alps, seeking enlightenment. After several months of dedicated practice of *zazen,* sitting meditation, with no discernible results, he impatiently confronted his *roshi.* "What does all this zen sitting, day and night in the *zendo,* have to do with enlightenment?" he asked the zen master. "It has as much to do with enlightenment," replied the wise mentor, "as it has to do with the sun rising in the morning." When the frustrated disciple heard his master's reply, he threw his hands into the air and asked with exasperation, "Then why should I continue to practice?" To which the zen master replied, "So that when the sun does rise, you will be awake." Similarly, the practice of holistic discernment is meant to keep us awake, so that when the Risen Son does appear in our life to guide us, we will not be caught dozing.

Holistic discernment is both an art and a gift. It is an art because we can, with practice, develop our ability to be more and more sensitive to the Spirit's movements in the whirl of our lives. Yet, ultimately, it is a gift because to be aware of and moved by God's presence depends totally on grace. Human effort alone cannot make it happen. All prayer is paradoxical in this way. Our efforts and dispositions are important, yet when we experience the mysterious movement of God in prayer, we know that it is not of our own doing; rather, grace has come upon us. Knowing this can help us to be earnest, yet relaxed, in our efforts. We simply try our best and trust in God to do the rest. In the process of discernment we attempt to be as wide open and undefended as possible so that when the wind of the Spirit comes, we will be sensitive to the slightest nudging of the divine breeze. When our lives are so propelled by the wind of the Spirit, we are living spiritual lives.

A story is told of concert pianist Rudolph Serkin, who was to perform Beethoven's "Apassionata Sonata" in Boston's Concert Hall one evening.[6] This was quite a daunting engagement, since the culturally sophisticated people of Boston have throughout the years been treated to the very best of the musical world. That evening, at the finish of Serkin's performance, there was an initial hush throughout the hall. Then, suddenly, a soft applause began, which gradually built to a loud, sustained applause. Next, the audience stood up in unison, as one person, and shouted its approval. Even that was not enough. People started to stand on their seats and shout out their praise. That evening Serkin's performance had transfixed the audience, which sensed that the man had become one with the music and the music had become one with the man. And what did Rudolph Serkin have to do with this? He practiced every day for eight hours. So, that evening, when the Spirit came, the vessel was ready. This story teaches us what it takes if we are to live with a discerning heart. Regular practice of discernment sharpens sensitivity to the creative Spirit hovering over our world. Living with a discerning heart requires ongoing practice, much like maintaining the proficiency of a concert pianist. At the height of his career Arthur Rubenstein, one of the world's most renowned concert pianists, said: "If I don't practice for one day, *I* know it. If I don't practice for two days, *the orchestra* knows it. If I don't practice for three days, *the whole world* knows it!" The same can be said for living spiritually attuned lives based on discernment. Like any other complex art, discernment cannot be learned offhand. To grasp the theme of God's presence and action amid the discordant notes of our lives requires a proficiency acquired through ongoing practice. When we "grasp the theme," we *get* what God is about in our life and are able to move harmoniously with the flow of grace. Life out of tune with the Spirit's voice leads to cacophony; life in tune with God's direction leads to harmony.

Conditions in the twenty-first century make living with a discerning heart very difficult. Modern technology, like e-mail, fax transmission, cell phones, instant messaging, and the like, speeds up the pace of life. While these innovations seemed at first to offer us more time for leisure and reflection, they have unexpectedly had the opposite effect. Our "saved time" is crammed with even more things to do. Rushed and busy lives, however, put us at risk of becoming spiritually insensitive and out of tune.

This book on holistic discernment offers a wide range of ways by which contemporary Christians can encounter God's presence and benefit from divine guidance to live meaningful and satisfying lives. The guidelines and approaches suggested here can serve as an aid to those who want to entrust their lives more fully to God by expanding the Spirit's sway in all they choose and do.

AN OVERVIEW

A brief overview of the structure of this book may be helpful. Chapter 1 views discernment both as a process of staying connected with God on life's journey and as a search for divine wisdom to guide us. Chapter 2 relies on Christian tradition and psychological sources to explore what a holistic approach to discernment entails. Chapter 3 highlights the need for a broad approach to discernment based on individual differences of personality, religious sensibilities, and ways of knowing. This chapter invites us to reflect on our own past experiences of discernment in order to understand how grace and temptation operate in our lives. Chapters 4, 5, and 6 discuss how our images of God, our desires, and our dreams can affect the search for God's guidance. Finally, Chapter 7 emphasizes the importance of ongoing fidelity to our personal path and following the Spirit's unique lead in our life, even in the face of fear.

I.

THE DISCERNING HEART

The art of awareness of God, the art of sensing His presence in our daily lives cannot be learned off-hand. God's grace resounds in our lives like a staccato. Only by retaining the seemingly disconnected notes comes the ability to grasp the theme.
—Abraham Joshua Heschel

DISCERNMENT REFERS TO BOTH a posture and a process. As a spiritual posture, discernment entails fostering a contemplative attitude that helps us to spot the presence of God in the concrete events and experiences of ordinary life. To live with a discerning heart is to believe, as Elizabeth Barrett Browning expressed it, that "earth's crammed with heaven" and that God is everywhere to be found in the holy ground of our existence.

As a process, discernment involves making decisions in a way that allows God to be a telling influence in our choices. The goal is to refine the acoustics of our heart so that we can better hear the Spirit's guidance. Discernment cultivates our ability to stay with the discordant notes of our lives with alertness and sensitivity until we are able to grasp the theme of what God is about with us. Thus, discernment is essential for spiritual living. When we are in tune with the rhythms of God's movements, we live in harmony with self, others, and the cosmos. When we are out of tune, our lives feel off-center, out of kilter. This chapter discusses two key aspects of discernment:

- Discernment as a commitment to stay connected to God and to listen to God's guidance on our journey of life; and
- Discernment as a search for wisdom.

A COMMITMENT TO A LIFELONG RELATIONSHIP WITH GOD

In his "First Principle and Foundation" meditation (*Spiritual Exercises*, no. 23), Ignatius of Loyola frames life as a journey that begins with God as the loving Source of life and ends with God as the loving Fulfillment of our being. We come from God and are meant to return to God. This Ignatian formulation echoes the poignant prayer of Augustine of Hippo: "You have made us for yourself, O God, and our hearts will remain restless until they rest in you." According to Christian spirituality, the human heart is created with a deep yearning for God. This built-in longing for the divine was placed there to assure that the trajectory of our journey on earth would stay steadily focused on its divine destination. George Herbert captures this belief beautifully in his poem "God's Pulley."

When God first made man,
Having a glass of blessings standing by;

Let us (said he) pour on him all we can:
Let the world's riches, which dispersed lie,
Contract into a span.

So strength first made a way;
Then beauty flow'd, then wisdom, honor, pleasure:
When almost all was out, God made a stay,
Perceiving that alone of all his treasure
Rest in the bottom lay.

For if I should (said he)
Bestow this jewel also on my creature,
He would adore my gifts instead of me,
And rest in Nature, not the God of Nature:
So both should losers be.

Yet let him keep the rest,
But keep them with repining restlessness:
Let him be rich and weary, that at least,
If goodness lead him not, yet weariness
May toss him to my breast.[1]

FAITHFUL LISTENING KEEPS US CONNECTED TO GOD ALONG THE WAY

Besides being the Source and Destiny of life, God also accompanies us on our human journey, hence the image of God as Emmanuel, literally meaning "God with us." Living with a discerning heart entails a commitment to stay in ongoing conversation with this mobile God, who walks with us in all the seasons of our lives. Biblical theologian Marcus Borg affirms the personal quality of God's presence to us when he states:

> I think God *"speaks"* to us. I don't mean oral or aural revelation or divine dictation. But I think God "speaks" to us—sometimes dramatically in visions, less dramatically in some of our dreams, in internal "prod-dings" or "leadings," through people, and through the devotional practices and scriptures of our tradition.

We sometimes have a sense—I sometimes have a sense—of being *addressed.*[2]

Discernment is a matter of listening to how we are being addressed by God. Or, as Henri Nouwen once put it, discernment is the movement from "absurdity to obedience." The word *absurdity* comes from the Latin *surdus,* meaning "deaf," and the word *obedience* comes from the Latin *ob-audire,* meaning "to listen." Discernment, then, is a life stance of being sensitively attuned to the promptings of Emmanuel. It schools us in living obedient lives.

The heart of obedience is a joyful yes to the good news that we are God's very own, chosen to be part of the family of God (Eph 1:14). Through obedience we affirm our familial relationship with God and express our desire to be influenced by God in our life choices. Naturally, as adults we are expected to use all of our abilities and resources to make the best plans for living full and loving lives. Yet, obedience invites us not only to let God influence the formulation of these plans, but also to stay in ongoing contact with God as we live them out.

The fluid nature of reality can bring about unexpected changes that require us to alter our original plans. Unexpected events—such as being laid off, the onset of chronic illness or disability, losing a spouse through death or divorce—can dramatically disrupt our lives and test our faith. If we give in to disillusionment or resist these changes, our suffering is compounded; but if we can look at what is happening with the eyes of faith, we will be open to the inherent call of God in the midst of our pain and struggle. An obedient attitude encourages us to accept reality as it is, even when it does not conform to our desires, and to make the best choices available to us so that we can continue to embrace life with hope and expectancy.

Internal changes can also have a disruptive effect on our plans, sometimes causing us to reevaluate our commitments and priorities. Getting a better handle on a compulsive need to please people, for example, can free us to make a truly free choice for the first time. We may come to realize that our original life commitment was not freely made because we were unconsciously pleasing our parents rather than following our heart. Or our original choice was an authentic one, but years later we find that we have changed so much that it no longer expresses our truest self. Or we may in midlife finally possess enough ego-strength to live out a deep desire or dream from our youth that was snuffed out by parental or peer disapproval. Whenever we find ourselves in such situations of unsettledness, the discerning question remains the same: What is the call of God in this experience?

A sports analogy illustrates nicely the dynamic nature of spiritual obedience, which requires that we journey nimbly on our path—always open, as were the three magi in search of the Christ child, to the ongoing directives of God. In football, each team is led by a quarterback who calls the plays during the huddle. The agreed-upon play determines how the offense will carry out its attempt to reach the goal for a touchdown. Sometimes, however, immediately before the ball is put into motion, the quarterback suddenly changes the play because he notices how the defensive team has positioned itself. This spontaneous change of play is called an *audible*. In real life, shifting circumstances often call for the same kind of adaptation and openness to change. To live spiritually vibrant lives requires staying receptively alert to the "audibles" that God calls out to us. Discernment trains us to hear God's audibles and to follow a new play. Spiritually awake or alert persons move into the future based on their ongoing experience of God's audibles. As a contemporary spiritual writer puts it, "No one is given complete information about divine will for themselves or for others. By giving us partial information, God invites us into deeper awareness of our core need to be in relationship."[3]

EXAMPLES OF FAITHFUL LISTENING

To be a discerning person is to imitate the response of Abraham, who heard the divine audible to change the course of his life. Out of obedience and undaunted by old age, he left the familiarity of family and homeland and proceeded into the unknown, trusting in the divine promise of a blessed future (Gen 12:1–5). To be a discerning person is to emulate the example of Mary when the angel of the annunciation announced a dramatic turning point in her life. Hearing the call of God, Mary understood the challenge before her: to give up her own plans for her future and to say a willing yes to her part in God's plan to make divine love incarnate in the world. In short, the angel Gabriel asked her to "let go and let God." After Gabriel's reassurance that she was deeply loved by God, Mary broke through her fear and resistance and uttered: "Body and soul I belong to God. Let it happen to me as you say" (Luke 1:38, J. B. Phillips' translation). In obedience, she surrendered trustingly to the sway of the Spirit in her life. Not being deaf to God's guiding voice, Abraham and Mary were both able to hear God's audible that announced a major departure from prearranged plans.

Contemporary Christians are similarly called to heed God's voice. As with Abraham and Mary, following God's lead entails a journey of faith and trust, often marked by ambiguity, uncertainty, and fear of the unknown. The story of Paul Mariani, an award-winning poet, critic, essayist, and holder of a chair in English at Boston College, provides a good illustration. After thirty-two years of teaching at the University of Massachusetts in Amherst, he found his life at a sudden crossroads as he wrestled with a cryptic call experienced in prayer, perhaps similar to the call delivered by the angel to Mary, to make a major change. His journal entry for Wednesday, January 5, 2000, during an individually directed retreat at a Jesuit spirituality center, recounts this annunciation moment.[4] Shortly after being caught completely off guard by his retreat director's question—Can you turn everything over to God?—he writes:

> "How can I?" I asked myself, climbing the dark stairs as I returned to my room....And then, like that, I found the grace somehow to say yes. "Why the hell not," I remember saying to myself. "Can I do any better than Him?" And then, suddenly, out of nowhere, the gentle command, *Go to BC*. Oddly, I've been following that directive ever since. The command was not, of course, what I'd been expecting, knowing no one at BC except a priest friend from the old days. In fact I'd never even seen the campus.

Mariani's perplexity paralleled that of Mary's when she protested to the angel Gabriel, "How can this be, since I am a virgin?" (Luke 1:34–35). And, as with Mary, the divine summons persisted:

> But there it was, the voice, *Go to BC*. After all these years at UMass, only to begin all over again at a Jesuit school. Why, I don't fully understand, but every time I have tried to shake the order off, something has steadied me. *This is what I want of you, Paul,* the voice seems to say, as it spoke to the prophets and to Christ. *It is*

enough for you to go. The rest will be made clear in due time.
Do not be anxious or worried.

This reassurance strangely resembled Gabriel's reassurance
of Mary and left Mariani with perhaps what Mary also experienced, lingering uncertainty!

> Well, isn't that what the Lord does, continually surpris-
> ing us if we will but leave listening room? And what if
> BC should turn out to have stood not for Boston Col-
> lege but Bard or—worse—British Columbia? I don't
> understand the full import here and keep thinking of
> the long trip from Montague to Chestnut Hill. Eighty-
> seven miles each way. And the long New England win-
> ters. I wonder if the prophets had a sense of humor. I
> know God must.

The next day's account describes a moment of consolation when he is moved to trust in God's love and faithfulness, and to keep moving, with hope, in the direction he
feels called to go. Returning from a meeting with his retreat
director, Mariani found himself "dwelling on God's thirst
for us, and of my lifelong thirst for Him. Why is it, in spite
of all my defiances," he wondered, "that He has never abandoned me? And why this fear of abandonment? *Why* should
God care so much about us as to pursue us down the ways?"
Then, filled with a renewed sense of God's loving largess
always offering us gift upon gift, he feels inspired to move
forward with hope and expectancy:

> At fifty-nine, one begins to think of cutting back, of
> doing less, and then of retirement. Why then do I keep
> feeling not as if I were about to close up shop but—like
> old Sarah in the Book of Genesis—as if I were on the
> verge of some great surprise?[5]

Though not quite as old as Abraham, who was seventy-five years old when he left Haran to embark on a new chapter in his life, Mariani's concern about making a major career shift at fifty-nine is something most people these days can share. Yet, his concern is calmed by a graceful intuition that, like Sarah who conceived and bore a son in old age (Gen 21:1–2), he too would be blessed with surprising fruitfulness.

Because the discernment process is subject to shifting subjective states and feelings, it is understandable how this experience of consolation could so easily be clouded over by doubt and fear the very next day:

> Then the nagging thought of going to Boston College and meeting the English department. And what if it should be *Thanks, but no thanks?* O.K. So be it. All I can do is present myself. It will be theirs to say yes or no. But then what was the calling really all about? An illusion? Am I jerking myself around for some reason too deep to fathom? Maybe there's a joke in all of this, after all. But if so, what's the point? And is there a point?[6]

As these dynamics of Mariani's discernment process make clear, the movement from absurdity to obedience is not one of quick clarity and sure answers. On Day Eighteen of his "long retreat," Mariani notes that even those who seriously discern a choice cannot shake off an ongoing wondering if the right decision was made. In the homily at a Mass Mariani attended, the priest spoke of his own difficulties in handing himself over to God. Once a hotdog pilot in World War II flying from the deck of the aircraft carrier *Essex,* he finally left the Navy, heard a call to return to school, and later, to be a Jesuit priest. Reflecting on the priest's life, Mariani writes:

Every step of the way he had to be led, always wondering if it was the right thing for him. Well, here he was, in his seventies, still trying to figure it out. And here I am—at fifty-nine—trying to do the same.[7]

Requiring patient trust and perseverance, discerning God's lead is a lifelong process.

DISCERNMENT AS A SEARCH FOR WISDOM

A second way in which discernment can be viewed is as a search for wisdom. The search for wisdom goes back to ancient times and persists strongly today. Paradoxically, at a time of "information glut," when more and more is available through the Internet and round-the-clock cable news, we seem to experience an ever greater need for wisdom. Facing the bewildering number of choices that confronts us, we long for some guiding wisdom. In the Judeo-Christian tradition, wisdom refers to two primary realities:

- First, it is "an experiential understanding of *how to live,* happily, deeply, in harmony with God, oneself, others, and the cosmos."[8]
- Second, it is understood as "a mystery into which one is invited to dwell ever more deeply—the very mystery of God present to us at the heart of reality, now manifest, now hidden, ever present but elusive, sustaining not only our own individual lives but the entire cosmos."[9] As the Book of Wisdom puts it, Wisdom, the feminine face of God,

> knows and understands all things,
> and she will guide me wisely in my actions
> and guard me with her glory. (Wis 9:11)

WISDOM AS EXPERIENTIAL KNOWLEDGE
ABOUT LIVING IN HARMONY

The first meaning of wisdom, understanding how to live in harmony with reality, comes to us mainly through experience, the school of hard knocks. As the Greek tragedian Aeschylus proclaimed repeatedly through the voice of his chorus, "wisdom comes through suffering." Suffering is part of the human condition and a necessary part of the growth process. Our attitude regarding our suffering determines whether we will be enriched by it or depleted by it. Suffering has some intrinsic value when it produces wisdom to guide our lives. Wisdom is the fruit of observation and reflection. It accumulates over the years, as we dwell with our experiences of love and labor, success and failure, to glean the lessons embedded there. And, more often than not, the painful experiences are the ones we linger with longest, trying to glean some redemptive value by mining them for helpful wisdom. Trial-and-error learning can disclose to us, in ways no book or expert consultant can, the personal wisdom that contains reliable guidelines for decision and choice. Self-knowledge based on personal experience reveals to us our unique mix of personal strengths and vulnerabilities, instincts and proclivities, impulses and habitual responses. Self-knowledge highlights our peculiar history of grace (the unique ways in which God typically leads us) and our history of temptation (the idiosyncratic ways in which we are typically deceived and misled) when making important decisions. This kind of self-knowledge provides an inner compass that can point out for us the true north of God's direction.

To garner wisdom from our experiences, especially painful ones, requires patience. Patience can be understood in both harmful and helpful ways in discernment. It can be harmful in two ways. First, patience can be used as an excuse to be apathetic, complacent, and inactive—the stance of a victim who is hopelessly overwhelmed. Second, patience can encourage a teeth-gritting, stoic endurance of pain based on a denial of the painful feelings that accompany a bad situation. Positively, as a helpful disposition in discernment, patience entails a commitment to be still in the midst of a painful situation until we understand what is going on.[10] This stance is counter-cultural, because the advertisements that saturate the media urge us to take advantage of innumerable ways (pills, thrills, cruises, and so on) to numb the pain quickly and move on. Unfortunately, these remedies provide quick relief from symptoms without preventing an equally quick recurrence of the pain because the root cause remains unexamined. Sometimes pain can be a friend, giving us a clue about something in our life that is not working and needs attention. Patient discernment encourages us to stay with the painful situation, not in an eyes-shut, "grin and bear it" way, but with attentiveness. Wakefulness in painful situations can provide valuable data for constructive change; it can increase our awareness of what we are feeling, what is causing the pain, what is not working, what is rubbing against the grain. Awareness of these things can be the beginning of a way out of dead ends and painful places because awareness leads to "response-ability," that is, the ability to respond.

This renewed sense of personal power to bring about life-giving changes enables us to journey with hope. Hope that things can be other than they are is critical at a time when what Thoreau observed years ago is more than ever true:

> The mass of men lead lives of quiet desperation. What is called resignation is confirmed desperation. A stereo-typed but unconscious despair is concealed even under what are called the games and amusements of

mankind....When we consider what...is the chief end of man,...it appears as if men had deliberately chosen the common mode of living because they preferred it to any others. Yet they honestly think there is no choice left.[11]

Patience, as a virtue, spawns hope, the often missing middle child of its theological siblings, faith and love. It is this hope that enables Christians to fight off the threat of living in "quiet desperation" and "unconscious despair."

The Chinese ideogram for patience conveys this positive understanding of patience (忍). The character is formed by placing "knife" (刃) on top of "heart" (心). Patience, then, is staying alert and attentive to that place in our life where something is causing pain in our heart. Armed with the awareness that comes with patient attentiveness, discernment unites us with the God of the Exodus, who gives us hope for release from stuck places. In this positive sense, patience is a virtue. It enables us to "not merely undergo experience, such as illness or loss, but actively *go through it*. We are not just passive victims of the crisis; we 'face' it. We can look into it searching out its meaning."[12]

BENEFITING FROM ACCUMULATED WISDOM

Other people's reflections, collected in wisdom traditions of various world religions and philosophies, also provide us with wisdom concerning how to live in harmony with reality. For example, the Taoist concept of *wu-wei*, the way of "non-doing," can contribute much to the process of holistic Christian discernment. In the arena of human action, *wu-wei* is a form of wisdom that allows a person who understands the dynamics of human affairs to use the least amount of energy to deal with them. This intelligence is not simply intellectual, states philosopher Alan Watts, but also the "unconscious intelligence of the whole organism and, in particular, the innate wisdom of the nervous system. *Wu-Wei* is a combination of this wisdom with taking the line of least resistance in all one's actions."[13]

While the "let's roll up our sleeves and get it done" mentality causes us to push and strain, *wu-wei* encourages us not to force things but instead to go with the flow, to roll with the punch, to swim with the current. Discussing the notion of fasting as refraining from a persistent need to figure things out, a contemporary spiritual writer states:

> [Fasting] can be understood to be about learning to give oneself ample space and time to focus. Before any big decision I want to give myself a whole week of not deliberating. If I give myself the gift of enough time without thinking and sorting, I can often come to a deeper awareness where a *choiceless* choice begins to emerge. Walt Whitman wisely said, "Loaf and invite your soul."[14]

Sometimes important decisions cannot be made because certain important variables remain unknown, or one's soul is not psychologically ready to move forward. Here the wisdom of *wu-wei* not to force things clearly applies. Many poor decisions are the results of an impatient impulse to put premature closure on a discernment process presently unable to yield a peaceful answer. The Greek New Testament uses two words for time: *chronos* and *kairos*. *Chronos* refers to clock time, time as the measure of motion. *Kairos* is the acceptable time of grace, the fullness of time intended by grace for something to happen. The wisdom of *wu-wei* corresponds with the biblical notion of *kairos*. Forced and rushed decisions run a high risk of error.

The wisdom of *wu-wei* also values flexibility. Alan Watts illustrates the way of non-doing with a comparison between a pine branch, which is hard and stiff, and a willow branch, which is soft and flexible. In a winter storm the heavy snow gathers on the pine branch until the mounting weight causes it to snap. The willow branch, on the other hand, yields to the weight of the snow and lets itself get pressed to the ground, where it gracefully unloads its oppressive burden and springs back to its natural position.[15] Of course, the willow's way is the path of effortless action. Thomas Merton, who was a devotee of Taoist wisdom, renders his own version of a traditional Taoist story that reveals the essence of *wu-wei:*

> When we wear out our minds, stubbornly clinging to one partial view of things, refusing to see a deeper agreement between this and its complementary opposite, we have what is called "three in the morning."
>
> What is this "three in the morning?"
>
> A monkey trainer went to his monkeys and told them: "As regards your chestnuts: you are going to have three measures in the morning and four in the afternoon."
>
> At this they all became angry. So he said: "All right, in that case I will give you four in the morning and three in the afternoon." This time they were satisfied.
>
> The two arrangements were the same in that the number of chestnuts did not change. But in one case the animals were displeased, and in the other they were satisfied. The keeper had been willing to change his personal arrangement in order to meet objective conditions. He lost nothing by it![16]

This story nicely illustrates the wisdom of *wu-wei*. The keeper had enough sense to recognize that the monkeys had their own reasons for wanting four measures of chestnuts in the morning and wasted neither time nor energy in stubbornly clinging to his original arrangement. By letting go, he was able to see things in perspective. And his accommodation to the monkeys caused only an accidental change; it did not affect the substance of his arrangement.

The *wu-wei* approach stems from Lao-tzu's famous words: "The Tao does nothing, and yet nothing is left undone."[17] Believers of Taoism know that these words are not to be taken literally or used to justify inertia, laziness, laissez-faire, or irresponsible passivity. Rather, *wu-wei* encourages relaxed and focused effort. A Taoist tale entitled "Cutting up an Ox" shows how *wu-wei* encourages a discerning approach to action, especially when we are confronted with resistance. The story is about a butcher who was so skillful at his craft that he used the same cleaver for nineteen years and managed to keep it as keen as if newly sharpened. When questioned about how he was able to cut up so many carcasses without dulling the blade, the butcher responded:

> There are spaces in the joints;
> The blade is thin and keen:
> When this thinness
> Finds that space
> There is all the room you need!
> It goes like a breeze!
> Hence I have this cleaver nineteen years
> As if newly sharpened!
>
> True, there are sometimes
> Tough joints. I feel them coming.
> I slow down, I watch closely
> Hold back, barely move the blade,
> And whump! the part falls away
> Landing like a clod of earth.
> Then I withdraw the blade,
> I stand still
> And let the joy of the work
> Sink in.

I clean the blade
And put it away.[18]

The butcher exemplifies the kind of patience required
when discerning appropriate action in conflictual situations. Unlike this wise butcher, compulsive achievers tend to
speed up their pace and double their efforts when faced
with opposition and hindrance. Instead of relying on force,
wu-wei suggests that we slow down, hold back, and watch
closely when encountering the "tough joints" in our lives.
Only such a contemplative approach will allow us to see the
"space" that will welcome our efforts.

WU-WEI AND THE UNFOLDING WAY

Wu-wei's philosophy of "not pushing the river" resonates
with the Quaker notion of waiting to see how the way
opens. "A Quaker method of discernment, which I consciously use often," writes Nancy Reeves, "is a combination
of listening for guidance and actively watching to see how
the Way opens. If I am receptive, I will see where Spirit is
leading me."[19] Central to this approach is the belief that
things will unfold as God intends. Some doors in the real
world will open up, and others will close. Watchful waiting,
as concrete realities and circumstance play out, can give us
an indication of how we are meant to proceed. When the
way opens, things effortlessly fall into place like dominos;
hospitable space welcomes our easy entry, like the butcher's
ox-cutting blade. This approach "means moving into align-
ment with God's will, getting with the divine flow. When
this occurs, the path naturally becomes clearer and
smoother. Cultivating the qualities of receptivity and flexibility is useful here and it may take time for way to open."[20]

WU-WEI AND CHRISTIAN WISDOM

A Christian understanding of *wu-wei* is reflected in the popular phrase "Let go and let God." This wise saying encourages us to trust deeply in the grace of God at work in our lives and serenely to let go of things that we cannot change at the present time. The path of *wu-wei* is based on the belief that the Tao, the principle of reality, is ultimately benevolent; we do not have to resist, or meddle, or interfere with the flow of life. Similarly, "letting go and letting God" rests on the conviction of faith that "all things work together for good for those who love God" (Rom 8:28). Of course, this faith relies on a contemplative attitude that recognizes God at work in all reality, laboring for our welfare.[21] Christian faith reassures us that because God raised Jesus from the dead, reality is ultimately gracious and God can be trusted. Thus, Christians are called to trust in the provident love of God and to go with the flow of God's grace, which "is able to accomplish abundantly far more than all we can ask or imagine" (Eph 3:20). Or, put colloquially, it is to believe that God always throws a better party! Relying on an image taken from Søren Kierkegaard, Marcus Borg comments that "faith is like floating in seventy thousand fathoms of water. If you struggle, if you tense up and thrash about, you will eventually sink. But if you relax and trust, you will float."[22] A *wu-wei* attitude in discernment stems from "trusting in the buoyancy of God...in the sea of being in which we live and move and have our being."[23] Believers who can relax and trust in God enough to wait for a way to open are more able to honor the wisdom of *wu-wei* than faithless and anxious people who cannot count on a gracious God to labor in their behalf.

WISDOM AS THE ABIDING PRESENCE
OF GOD STEEPED IN MATTER

The second meaning of wisdom points to the world as a "divine milieu," in which, as Teilhard de Chardin reminds us, "the divine influence [is] secretly diffused and active in the depths of matter."[24] Christian discernment encourages us to be attentive to the mystery of God present to us in the heart of reality, ever present yet elusive as we make life choices. According to Christian faith our lives can be guided by the divine influence that actively abides in all creation when we earnestly seek the will of God. Based on this conviction, Ignatius of Loyola encouraged those making the spiritual exercises in search of God's will to enter the experience with openness and generosity. He assured them that if they brought their struggles and questions in an honest and open way into the retreat and gave themselves generously and wholeheartedly to the experience, they would experience a unique Providence entering and disposing of their lives according to divine Wisdom. This Ignatian guideline for finding God's will during a retreat can profitably be extended to the whole of life. If we approach all of our ordinary experiences with the same open and expectant attitude that God's wisdom will in some mysterious way manifest itself to us in the innumerable threads that make up the web of our daily lives, we will enhance our ability to recognize God's guidance. Faith expands our readiness to see and to hear. Faith-filled eyes are alert to the guiding hand of God, whether it comes in the form of a book title that catches our eyes when browsing at Barnes and Noble, a friend's passing comment, a dream, or a word or image that leaps out of a page we are reading. For Ignatius, God's all-pervasive presence is neither impersonal nor inert, but dynamically at work in all creation in our behalf. Discernment helps us to detect the benevolent movements of God in our life so that our decisions and choices can move with the currents of grace.

DISCERNMENT OF SPIRITS

An important aspect of discernment is the ability to distinguish among the various spirits that buffet our lives, for not all winds are Pentecostal ones ushering in God's Spirit. Other winds may be fanned by spirits that are contrary to God's desires. The concept of spirits allows for a variety of understandings. Medieval theologians, in their angelology, bestowed an ontological reality on these good and bad spirits. Commenting on Ignatius of Loyola's use of the terms "good spirit" and "bad spirit," Ernest Larkin writes:

> The theology of the *Exercises* is not dependent on Ignatius' medieval world-view of angels and devils. His use of the two spirits struggling for dominance in the soul is the imagery of the times. But the meaning is the biblical struggle between...grace and sin...the inevitable war between the forces of good and evil. Ignatius' angelology and demonology are beside the point.[25]

Thus, Ignatius's historically conditioned language should not distract modern readers.

Some modern interpreters prefer to understand these spirits as contrary psychic states within the human personality: the good spirit as that which is oriented to God, and the evil or bad as that which sabotages the human's longing for God. In his Letter to the Romans, Saint Paul paints a psychological self-portrait that has become a classical illustration of our condition as human beings. The passage has an enduring ring because its description of Paul's inward struggle resonates deeply with the personal experience of people throughout the ages. Like Paul, we too live with a divided self. We encounter warring forces within ourselves so strong and autonomous that we often feel helpless and weak. Like Paul, we are perplexed by the mystery of our interior fragmentation. We know what the apostle means when he declares in frustration: "I cannot understand my own actions. For I do not do what I want, but I do the very thing I hate....I can will what is right, but I cannot do it. For I do not do the good I want, but the evil I do not want is what I do....Wretched man that I am!" (Rom 7:14, 18, 24). Self-sabotaging tendencies wage war within every man and woman. That is why the process of discernment must provide ways of distinguishing among these spirits.

According to Saint Paul, we are called to let the Spirit of God *(pneuma)* hold sway while resisting the oppositional pull of the "flesh" *(sarx)*. In his Letter to the Galatians, he tells us that we can tell which spirit is influencing our behavior and choices by the concrete ways our lives are affected.

> Let me put it like this: if you are guided by the Spirit you will be in no danger of yielding to self-indulgence, since self-indulgence is the opposite of the Spirit, the Spirit is totally against such a thing, and it is precisely because the two are so opposed that you do not always carry out your good intentions....When self-indulgence is at work, the results are obvious: fornication, gross indecency and sexual irresponsibility; idolatry and sorcery; feuds and wrangling, jealousy, bad temper and quarrels; disagreements, factions, envy; drunkenness, orgies and similar things....What the Spirit brings is very different: love, joy, peace, patience, kindness, goodness, trustfulness, gentleness and self-control. (Gal 5:16–23)

This passage from Paul represents the perennial wisdom of Christianity regarding how to determine which spirit is holding sway over us. Paul's first-century teaching was echoed in the sixteenth-century guidelines of Saint Ignatius for distinguishing between the "good spirit" (Paul's *pneuma*) and the "bad spirit" (Paul's *sarx*). For those who are sincerely trying to live loving lives, Ignatius states that God will guide them through experiences of consolation, which manifests itself as any increase in faith, hope, love, a deeper capacity to trust, a sorrow for one's sins, and an increased desire for joyful and loving service.[26] Clearly, Ignatian consolation parallels the Pauline fruits of the Holy Spirit—love, joy, peace, patience, kindness, goodness, trustfulness, gentleness, and self-control. In the common teaching of Paul and Ignatius we find a concrete way of searching for the wisdom of God's Spirit in the many choices we face.

Unfortunately, Paul's helpful norm for distinguishing among the spirits was distorted through the centuries by a misunderstanding of his teaching. In his letters Paul set "spirit" in opposition to "flesh" (*sarx* in Greek), not "body" (*soma* in Greek). However, many Christians through the years have wrongly interpreted Paul by setting spirit against body. For Paul, *flesh* was an abstraction that summed up all the forces that are inimical to the spirit, the sinful element in human nature. Contemporary descriptions of flesh as a spirit antithetical to the Spirit of God include:

- the spirit of resentment and revenge
- the spirit of blind ambition
- the spirit of ruthless competition
- the spirit of selfishness and narcissism
- the spirit of pleasure-idolizing hedonism
- the spirit of prejudice and condemnation
- the spirit of hatred and cruelty

Paul's use of "flesh" certainly did not refer to the physical aspect of our existence, our concrete bodies. To equate flesh with our bodies makes everything associated with the body negative and suspect: our sexuality, affectivity, and sensuality. When tied to flesh, these valuable aspects of our embodiment are made guilty by association. This misunderstanding accounts for the various strands of Christian spirituality that devalue the human body and dismiss the importance of considering bodily indications of God's lead, such as sensations of tension or ease, and feeling states of excitement and joy or of depression and listlessness. A central thesis of this work on discernment is that a discernment process that neglects the data of the physical self is seriously flawed. But more will be said on this subject later when discussing the importance of heeding the wisdom of the body in Christian discernment.

The story of Jesus' healing of a deaf man (Mark 7:31–37) provides a biblical illustration of God's involvement with us as we strive to grow in discernment, that is, to move from being deaf to being able to hear. One day, some people brought to Jesus a man who was both deaf and dumb; they asked for a cure. Jesus gently led the man to a private location where they could be alone. Putting his fingers into the man's ears and touching his tongue with spittle, Jesus looked prayerfully up to heaven and sighed. Then he said to the man, "Ephphatha," that is "Be opened." At that point, the man was cured and spoke clearly. That Jesus sighed indicates effort and exertion on the part of Jesus as he helped the man to hear. This story reminds us of the good news that the risen Jesus continues to be at work laboring to help us hear the voice of the Spirit. Holistic discernment reminds us that our efforts to hear are always aided by Jesus the healer.

To sum up, being persons of spiritual discernment entails a twofold commitment: (1) to stay connected to a mobile

God, who walks with us, and to listen to God's guidance as we navigate our journey; and (2) to seek divine wisdom that is embedded in the accumulated wisdom of our past, as well as in the ongoing promptings of the Spirit dwelling in our hearts as we seek to live happily and deeply in harmony with God, self, and others.

Personal Reflections and Spiritual Exercises

Consulting Your Personal Compass[27]

At any given point in our lives we experience a mixture of desires, urges, and longings that stir our energies in one direction or another. Some of these psychic energies are compatible and allow us to move in a single direction in living them out. Others are conflicting and require us to choose among them: to let go of one thing in order to embrace another; to say goodbye to something in order to say hello to something new.

The image of a personal compass is helpful because a compass lays out the different directions open to us, and its circular form, like the symbol of a mandala, encompasses all the pushes and pulls within our inner self. Thus, consulting our personal compass can help us clarify the direction in which we need to move to achieve greater balance and wholeness, healing and spiritual enrichment.

1. On a piece of drawing paper, draw a circle and divide the circle into four quadrants, representing the four directions. Leave an area in the center of the circle open.

2. In each of the quadrants draw or write the events, choices, images, questions, and so on, that fit that direction. Some may prefer to use magazine pictures and the copy that accompanies advertisements to express the various urgings of the heart.

The following suggestions are guidelines for each direction:

EAST: The direction of the rising sun.

—What new energy and/or movement is starting to emerge
  in you?
—What is starting to happen and what are you taking hold
  of?
—Where are you being called to embrace something new?
—Are you aware of issues or areas in need of healing or
  change?

WEST: The direction of the setting sun, the direction of
endings and letting go.

—What or who needs to be released, ended, shed?
—What beliefs, attitudes, and so forth do you need to die
  to?
—What maps no longer work for your life?
—Where is deep healing needed?

NORTH: The North Star represents your guiding light,
the stabilizing force, your spiritual values, mentors, and
so on.

—Who deeply loves and guides you?
—What images of God nurture and sustain you?
—Who are your spiritual guides and dearest friends?

SOUTH: The direction of sunny exposure. This direction is marked by your lively energy, imagination, and
spontaneity.

—Where is your creative energy being called forth?
—What do you really long to do or be?
—How do you nurture yourself?
—About what hobbies are you passionate?

In the CENTER draw your image of an unconditional YES to
your life, to living it fully. What would a full yes to God in your
whole person, physically, mentally, and spiritually look like?

3. When completed, spend some time in reflection and prayer with your personal life compass. Journal your thoughts, ideas, struggles, and feelings.

—Where are you saying yes?
—Where are you struggling?

You may wish to return to your compass many times in prayer and reflection to allow it to reveal more fully the insights and information that are there for you.

II.
REFINING THE
ACOUSTICS OF THE HEART

Listen carefully...with the ear of your heart.
—Prologue, *Rule of Saint Benedict*

It is only with the heart that one sees rightly;
what is essential is invisible to the eyes.
—Antoine de Saint Exupery,
The Little Prince

To know something important "by heart" is an experience
of wholeness. The term *heart* is a traditional image for a way
of perceiving, feeling, and loving that engages the total person. To Saint Augustine, the word signifies "our whole interior and spiritual life, and it includes mind and will,
knowledge and love."[1] Heart, when used to symbolize spiritual discernment, indicates that following God is not something primarily heady, action oriented, or moralistic.
Rather, it is a matter of being caught up in a dynamic loving
relationship with God and others. A heart-centered
approach to discernment is holistic.

In the New Testament the word *holistic* (from the Greek
holus) means "total" or "whole," as in the story of the widow's
mite, in which Jesus commends the woman for putting her

holon ton biov (all she had to live on) into the treasury (Mark 12:44). Like the dance called the hokey pokey, which invites us to "put your whole self in," holistic discernment invites us to put our whole self into the process. A holistic approach is inclusive and takes seriously the knowledge-bearing capacity not only of the mind but also of the body, emotions, senses, imagination, feelings, intuition, and dreams. "Two fundamentally different ways of knowing interact to construct our mental life," states psychologist Daniel Goleman. "One, the rational mind, is the mode of comprehension we are typically conscious of: more prominent in awareness, thoughtful, able to ponder and reflect. But alongside that there is another system of knowing: impulsive and powerful, if sometimes illogical—the emotional mind."[2] The research findings in the field of neurology, Goleman argues, show that how well we do in life is determined by both rational and emotional intelligence. "The old paradigm," he states, "held an ideal of reason freed of the pull of emotion. The new paradigm urges us to harmonize head and heart."[3]

Holistic discernment revolves around a form of knowing that goes beyond cold rationality. This mode of knowing is reflected in the Hebrew verb *yadah*, signifying the kind of intimate knowledge resulting from the unification of intellect, feeling, and actions. Ignatian spirituality speaks of it as *sentir*, a felt knowledge that pervades the whole of one's being. As Paul Tillich puts it, it is not so much "grasping the truths of faith," but "being grasped by the Truth of faith." In his autobiography C. S. Lewis provides a vivid description of a time when philosophical and intellectual constructs of Christianity came to life for him in this holistic way of knowing:

> As the dry bones shook and came together in that
> dreaded valley of Ezekiel's, so now a philosophical the-

orem cerebrally entertained, began to stir and heave and throw off its gravecloths, and stood upright and became a living presence. I was to be allowed to play at philosophy no longer....Total surrender, the absolute leap in the dark, were demanded.[4]

Holistic knowing enables us to "listen to the messages from all the self's aspects: the mind, the heart, the genitals, the viscera, the spiritual sensitivities."[5] Various forms of existential therapy value this holistic mode of knowing; these therapies try to restore the place of feelings where rationality has been the exclusive mode of operating. Gestalt therapy, for example, "undercuts language, the tool of thought, and clears the way for an approach that is explicitly *organismic*."[6]

An organismic approach is holistic because it places the body, with its movement and sensations, on the same level as the mind and its abstract thoughts and verbal symbols. This approach recognizes the body-spirit or psychosomatic unity of the person and affirms that bodily expressions often reveal interior states pertinent to making a choice. Hardly an esoteric concept, the psychosomatic unity of the person can be observed whenever bodily reactions reveal affective states. Blushing, sweaty palms, and accelerated heart rate are common examples of these physical manifestations of emotions. Gestalt therapists, for example, rely heavily on body language for an indication of psychological states. They generally believe that the body conveys how a person feels more truthfully than words. Because our bodily posture and gestures often unconsciously express our interior states, awareness of them can reveal what is going on in us.

Gestalt therapist James Simkin recounts a case that illustrates this organismic approach. Once, when working with a man struggling to decide whether to remain in a business venture recently begun with a friend, Simkin asked the client to imagine sticking with his business commitment. As the client imagined concretely what this option would entail, Simkin directed him to attend to his bodily sensations. When he imagined remaining with the business, the client's stomach tied up in knots. Then Simkin directed him to fantasize dropping the commitment. As the client did so, his stomach began to unravel and relax. The therapist then asked him to continue to shuttle between the two different fantasies, while simultaneously paying attention to his bodily reactions. As the client did so, he discovered a recurrent pattern: whenever he imagined staying with the business venture, his body was filled with stress; whenever he imagined abandoning the business deal, his body began to relax. Simkin concludes:

> Being able to self-validate what is the correct solution through one's own body language is a tremendous help in the economy of psychotherapy. Many of the transference and countertransference difficulties can be avoided, as well as the pitfalls of interpretation, through teaching oneself and one's patients how to use their symptoms—how to listen to their own body language.[7]

Simkin's case demonstrates how useful the data produced by the imagination, senses, bodily sensations, and feelings can be in decision-making. "My total organismic sensing of a situation is more trustworthy than my intellect," states psychologist Carl Rogers in support of a holistic approach. Testifying to this "wisdom of the organism," Rogers states: "As I gradually come to trust my total reactions more deeply, I find that I can use them to guide my thinking....I think of it as trusting the totality of my experience, which I have learned to suspect is wiser than my intellect. It is fallible I am sure, but I believe it to be less fallible than my conscious mind alone."[8]

ATTENTION TO INTERIOR MOVEMENTS

What psychologists such as Rogers and Simkin say of decision-making is equally true of discernment. A holistic approach to discernment maintains that we must be alert to how we are being touched by God in all areas of our lives, because no aspect escapes the influence of the divine Spirit. When thought is the coin of the realm, other important sources of information, like feelings, bodily reactions, and intuitions, can be overlooked. A purely rational approach to discernment is impoverished because it fails to recognize God's influence in religious and affective experiences. Like holistic decision-making, good discernment must take into account one's total, organismic sensing of a situation. A society dominated by science and technology often mistrusts feelings and touts a coldly dispassionate approach as the only intelligent way to make decisions. Nevertheless, recent neurological findings have verified what common sense has told us long ago: feelings have a crucial role in navigating the endless stream of decisions we must make for satisfying living.

> While strong feelings can create havoc in reasoning, the *lack* of awareness of feeling can also be ruinous, especially in weighing the decisions on which our destiny largely depends: what career to pursue, whether to stay with a secure job or switch to one that is riskier but more interesting, whom to date or marry, where to live, which apartment to rent or house to buy—and on and on through life. Such decisions cannot be made well through sheer rationality; they require gut feeling, and the emotional wisdom garnered through past

experiences. Formal logic alone can never work as the basis for deciding whom to marry or trust or even what job to take; *these are realms where reason without feeling is blind* (emphasis added).[9]

Ignatian spirituality goes further in asserting the importance of feelings by connecting our emotional awareness with our ability to decipher how we are being moved by God. Ignatius "came to recognize that human experiences of joy and desolation, of enthusiasm and depression, of light and darkness, are not just human emotions which vary like the wind in a storm, but are the means by which we recognize the movements within our spirit stirred by the Spirit of Jesus."[10] Thus, in the *Spiritual Exercises* Ignatius instructs the director of a retreat to focus on the interior movements and experiences of the retreatant. If the retreatant reports not being affected by any movements, either of consolation or desolation, it is important that the director inquire into this (no. 6). For Ignatius, the director's central question to the retreatant throughout the experience of the *Spiritual Exercises* is: "How were you *moved* in prayer?"

INTEGRATING REASON, AFFECT, AND RELIGIOUS EXPERIENCE

Ignatius's approach to discerning life choices reflects the organismic approach of Gestalt therapy and can be considered as an early form of holistic decision-making. Like the organismic approach of Gestalt therapy, Ignatian guidelines for deciding or "making an election" emphasize the integration of thought, affectivity, imagination, and sensation. Ignatius's *sentir* or felt knowledge is equivalent to Gestalt therapy's idea of "emotional insights."[11] These emotional insights help decision-making because they are based on an expanded awareness of one's relationship with the environment, accompanied by positive feelings and a sense of discovery.[12] For example, when an obese person is able to persevere in a weight-loss program for an extended period, he may happily discover that his power to control his eating is greater than he had thought. Or a student struggling with self-doubts may realize, with the help of a counselor, that her consistent success in science and mathematics classes makes it realistic for her to dream about being a physician like her mother. These examples of emotional insights differ greatly from purely intellectual insights that have no impact on life decisions because they are not rooted in one's actual experiences. The case cited by Simkin above is a clear illustration of how Gestalt therapists lead clients to emotional insight by teaching them how to attend to their actual bodily reactions and emotions when deciding. In a similar way, Ignatius attempts to help retreatants making a decision detect God's influence as it impinges on their minds, hearts, and bodies.

IGNATIUS'S THREE TIMES OF MAKING AN ELECTION

In the *Spiritual Exercises* Ignatius describes three times or ways in which God can guide people faced with choice. The first time occurs when God "so moves and attracts the will that a devout soul without hesitation, or the possibility of hesitation, follows what has been manifested to it" (no. 175). Ignatius cites the responses of Saint Paul and Saint Matthew to Christ's call in order to illustrate this first time of election. Phenomenologically, this first time can be viewed as a moment of peak religious experience when individuals feel overwhelmed by an inner sense of certainty about their decisions. At such moments they may experience something deep within "click into place," providing an intuitive sense of how they must proceed. Everything points in one direction, and they feel no contrary movement. Or they may perceive such a total congruence between their sense of internal requiredness (what they feel they must do) and God's will (what they think God wants of them) that the course to be followed is unambiguously clear. Sometimes, quite apart from any deliberation, a personal "moment of truth" can spring suddenly upon the person without any antecedent cause, like a forceful flash of insight, removing any further need for deliberating.[13]

The second time of decision-making suggested by Ignatius emphasizes the knowledge-bearing capacity of feelings. It occurs when individuals must rely on their affective states of consolation or desolation to detect the influence of God regarding the decision to be made (no. 176). In the case of people progressing earnestly along the spiritual path,[14] Ignatius understands consolation as a complex of positive feelings that encourages, supports, and confirms a prospective decision as being "right." He sees desolation as a complex of negative feelings that discourages, questions, and calls into doubt a prospective decision, suggesting that it is "not right." The assumption underlying this second time of election is that emotions can be indicators of God's guidance.

The third time of decision-making highlights the process of reasoning (nos. 177–87).[15] Picturing oneself on one's deathbed and recalling God's purpose for creating us (that we might live in loving relationship with God by praising, reverencing, and serving God [no. 23]), the person is asked to list the pros and cons of various options (no. 186). This third time presupposes that God's guiding influence can be felt in the process of reasoning.[16] Like the values-clarification exercise that asks people what they would do if they had only a week to live, this Ignatian method relies on the truth that can come at death's door to provide a perspective for present choices. In other words, it asks people to anticipate which decision they would ratify or regret when facing death. In this third time of election Ignatius also provides an example of heeding one's inner wisdom when he suggests imagining a person coming to us for help in making a choice similar to one we are facing. We should listen carefully to what we counsel this person to do and then follow our own advice (no. 185). This Ignatian exercise contains a twofold value: it increases clarity through objectification (telling our own story in the third person) and it encourages us to honor our inner authority.[17]

The genius of Ignatius, theologian Michael J. Buckley points out, was not that he counted transpersonal influences, or the attractions of affectivity, or the process of thinking as critical factors in securing the guidance of God. Others also shared this inclusive view. Ignatius's explanation of the dynamics of these three, often interrelating, factors within a person's religious experience is unique. "What Ignatius provided," maintains Buckley, "was a structure within which each of these finds a significant place; none is dismissed out of hand. A coordination among them is established so that they reach an integrity of effect and one is taught how to recognize and reply to each."[18]

CHOICE AND CONFIRMATION:
THE TWOFOLD IGNATIAN DYNAMIC

The phrase *integrity of effect* aptly describes the desired outcome of Ignatian discernment. Presuming the person is genuinely committed to doing the will of God and is free from inordinate attachments that destroy freedom, the decision is integral if it emanates from an integration of feelings and thoughts. Ignatius sought this integration by building into the second and third times of decision-making a complementary dynamic. He directs the person who makes a decision based on the rational approach of the third time to seek affective confirmation by prayerfully attending to his or her feelings as suggested by the second time of election (no. 183). In other words, following a decision the person should stay in close touch with the feelings that arise as a result of the decision and determine whether they confirm the rightness of the choice or cast doubt on it. After a period of testing, if positive feelings (for example, peace, joy, hope, confidence) dominate, it is clear that affectivity has joined with intelligence to produce a harmonious effect. However, if negative and disturbing feelings (such as doubt, fear, anxiety, discouragement) persist, then a closure would seem premature and the person should continue the process until an inner harmony is produced through the alliance of head and heart.

Conversely, a person who makes a decision based on the affective approach of the second time should also seek rational confirmation through a method of the third time. William Peters, in his commentary on the *Spiritual Exercises,* cites the *Directory of 1599* to substantiate this point. He notes that Juan de Polanco, a close friend of Ignatius, called the second time of election "more excellent" than the third, but adds that it might be wise to check the result of an election made in this time by one of the methods of the third.[19] Concretely speaking, when we make a decision based on a pattern of consolation surrounding a specific choice, we are still encouraged to strengthen that choice by thinking of all the pros that support that choice. At this point in the discernment process, we should play down the cons and put them on the back burner and not permit them to sabotage the decision that has just been made peacefully through consoling experiences in prayer. This approach allows us to invest wholeheartedly in the direction we have chosen in consolation without being hampered by any nagging voice of negativity. Of course, we need to monitor our ongoing experiences of consolation or desolation as we actually live out our choice in order to confirm its rightness or wrongness in concrete experience.[20] Choice and confirmation make up the two-part dynamic of the Ignatian method of discernment.

Clearly, the second time of decision-making based on affectivity, and the third time, based on reasoning, were designed by Ignatius to function in a complementary dynamic. The Ignatian process seeks to ground life choices on felt knowledge, not on theoretical abstractions. This process, according to Ignatian scholar John Futrell, involves paying attention simultaneously to "the continuity of thoughts during reflection, the concomitant feelings constantly reacting to these thoughts—feelings which confirm or call into question the orientation of the reflection—and the growing understanding which involves both the thoughts and feelings—felt-knowledge."[21]

GROUNDING IGNATIUS'S THREE TIMES
OF ELECTION IN CONTEMPORARY THOUGHT

Ignatius's first time or way of making an election, when a person is so touched by God that he or she knows deeply the path to be followed without any need for deliberation, finds contemporary support in the distinction made between religious truth and scientific truth. Whereas truth-claims in science need to be backed up by reproducibility, a religious truth may be based on a single, unique, irrepeatable religious experience. According to the scientific method, a truth-claim can be empirically verified only if an experiment produces the same results over and over again under the same conditions or variables. A religious truth, however, requires no such reproducibility to establish its claim to validity.

According to psychologist Joseph R. Royce, "The scientific enterprise is objective and it moves in the direction of making generalizations. Religion, on the other hand, demands personal involvement or subjectivity....It recognizes that such individual involvement may be unique rather than a general phenomenon."[22] Existential validation, not empirical verification, grounds a religious truth. Existential validation occurs when we experience deeply the meaning, significance, and well-being produced by what we know through a religious experience. Theologian Paul Tillich illustrates how such a religious truth can come in a powerful experience of being "struck by grace":

> Do you know what it means to be struck by grace?...We cannot transform our lives, unless we allow them to be transformed by the stroke of grace. It happens or it does not happen. And certainly it does not happen if we try to force it upon ourselves, just as it shall not happen so long as we think, in our self-complacency, that we have no need of it. Grace strikes us when we are in great pain and restlessness. It strikes us when, year after year, the longed-for perfection of life does not appear, when despair destroys all joy and courage. Sometimes at that moment a shaft of light breaks into our darkness, and it is as though a voice were saying: "You are accepted. You are accepted," accepted by that which is greater than you, and the name of which you do not know. Do not ask for the name now, perhaps you will find it later. Do not try to do anything; do not

perform anything; do not intend anything. Simply
accept the fact that you are accepted. If that happens
to us, we experience grace....Sometimes it happens
that we receive the power to say "yes" to ourselves, that
peace enters into us and makes us whole, that self-
hatred and self-contempt disappear, and that our self is
reunited with itself. Then we can say that grace has
come upon us.[23]

Tillich's description of the experience of being struck by
grace resembles Ignatius's description of consolation without a previous cause. "I said without previous cause," states
Ignatius, "that is, without any preceding perception or
knowledge of any subject by which a soul might be led to
such a consolation through its own acts of intellect and will"
(no. 330). Like Tillich's description of grace, this consolation described by Ignatius is characterized by its total gift
nature. Unlike scientific knowledge that is engendered by a
controlled experiment, religious knowledge is simply
received as a gift from God. "It belongs solely to the Creator
to come into a soul, to leave it, to act upon it, to draw it
wholly to the love of His Divine Majesty," states Ignatius in
his "Rules for Discernment of Spirits" (no. 330). Those who
make an election in Ignatius's first time have clearly been
struck by an amazing grace that eliminates the need for any
discernment process, since they sense deep within, without
any doubt or contrary inner movement, the course they
must pursue.

However, when such an experience of consolation is not
accompanied by a deep clarity about choices to be made, it
is critical to note Ignatius's caveat that people who have
experienced consolation without a previous cause "must
consider it very attentively, and must cautiously distinguish
the actual time of the consolation from the period which

follows it. At such a time the soul is still fervent and favored with the grace and aftereffects of the consolation which has passed. In this second period the soul frequently forms various resolutions and plans which are not granted directly by God" (no. 336). In this time of "after glow," the plans and choices we make cannot be attributed directly to God, as was the actual moment of consolation, but have their source in our own fallible human reasoning and judgments. As such, they are susceptible to error.

Ignatius's three times of making an election can also be further understood in light of the theological distinction between God's transcendent and immanent nature. This distinction underpins his three ways of being influenced by God in our discernment. The first time of election highlights the transcendent nature of God, while the second and third times of election emphasize the immanent nature of God. When we refer to God's transcendence, we are acknowledging the fact that God is illimitable Mystery, totally beyond and dissimilar to any created reality and far beyond our human comprehension. Sovereign over all of creation, God can intervene in our lives to influence our choices without the mediation of thoughts, feelings, and images. When we speak of God's immanence, we acknowledge that God communicates to us not through mystical or ecstatic experiences alone, but also through the normal human faculties of knowing and experiencing. When we acknowledge that God is both transcendent and immanent, we affirm God's indwelling presence within the world while maintaining that God is wholly other and irreducible to any aspect of creation.

A DISCERNMENT PROCESS BASED ON THE IGNATIAN TRADITION

IDENTIFY the decision that faces us or the issue we need to resolve

EXAMINE the underlying values (human, Christian, spiritual) and personal concerns involved

Through reflection, we clarify the values that are at stake in the decision (values clarification) and ask whether they are worth pursuing (value critique).

STRIVE for Ignatian indifference

Ignatian indifference is a state of inner freedom, openness, and balance that allows us beforehand not to incline more toward one option than to another, but to allow our preference be shaped by the single criterion of what will enhance our ability to love God and to embody that love for others in the concrete context of our lives.

Not easy to attain, indifference is a poised freedom that preserves our ability to go one way or another depending on the indication of God's lead. By calling for indifference, Ignatius is calling for a willingness right from the start to be influenced in the process by God's guidance.

Unfortunately, *indifference* is a bad choice of a word to convey Ignatius's meaning, since it often connotes apathy and complacency. For Ignatius, it has nothing to do with the absence of feelings; nor does it mean disinterest in people and situations. The sculpture of the discus thrower is a helpful image in understanding Ignatian indifference. Manifesting taut muscles ready to be sprung and pent-up energy ready to be released, the statue captures at once the paradoxical combination of action and rest. It is as if the discus thrower has been caught at a moment when he is ready to hurl the discus but is in waiting. Similarly, Ignatian indifference calls for a spiritual posture that imitates that of the discus thrower. We are called to be ever ready to embody the love of God in any way we can, but we must have the inner discipline to wait and to withhold action until we get an indication of directionality from God.

If unable to achieve indifference, discussing the matter in spiritual direction can help us understand what we are struggling with and what the next peaceful step might be in our discernment.

TAKE time to pray over the matter, paying attention to how we are being drawn or led

This moves our reflection into the context of prayer; we ask for God's guidance and try to be sensitive to how we are being drawn when the matter is brought to prayer.

Here it is important to remember what was said above regarding the interplay of reason, affect, and religious experience in the decision-making process. God can influence us through our thoughts as well as through our feelings of consolation and desolation in prayer.

MAKE a choice based on both the results of our "head work" and our "heart work"

"Head work" includes weighing the matter with our reasoning process by which we research the relevant information, consult with resource persons when necessary, listen to all the different aspects of our being (needs, wants, desires, and so on), and consider the pros and cons of the different options.

"Heart work" entails sitting with the choice that our reasoning has determined to be the best and checking for affective confirmation, that is, whether our feelings go along with what our mind has decided. If, over a period of time, the feelings that surround the choice we have made are predominantly enlivening and positive (Ignatian "consolation"), we can consider this a sensible way to proceed. If, however, the feelings are predominantly stifling and negative (Ignatian "desolation"), then we must keep the process open until we can arrive at a decision that head and heart can jointly embrace.

The feelings we are monitoring here are not the fleeting feelings that are our immediate responses to stimuli that impinge upon us throughout the day. That level of feelings is like the fluctuating waves on the surface of the ocean. The feelings that are relevant to this process of affective confirmation are similar to the more stable currents between the surface and bottom of the ocean. This mid level of feelings is more constant and stable and thus more relevant in determining whether our feelings confirm or call into question the decision we have made through our thinking process.

Addressing the importance of this affective confirmation, Pierre Wolff articulates a theological affirmation that is central to the Ignatian approach: "Within ourselves, by the process of discernment we offer the results of our intellectual search to the Spirit. If our Divine Guest indicates agreement with us through enlivening echoes produced at the core of our being, we may say that, at that level, we and the Spirit are in tune with one another and that we are deciding *together* our will. What we want at this depth is what God wants for us: God's will for us is what we decide."[24]

DISCUSS the matter with a spiritual companion

Because discerning the movements of God can often be a complex task requiring assistance, this step calls for sharing our deliberation with a trusted friend, counselor, or minister—someone who is committed to helping us be truthful, patient, and persevering in our search for God's call. Because we are all liable to self-deception, we need help to be objective and honest.

DIALOGUE with those who will be intimately affected by the decision being made

Too often decisions that affect spouses, children, and other loved ones are made unilaterally, without engaging the participation of those who have a right to be involved. These decisions, for example, may pertain to changing jobs, selling the house and moving, or caring for aging parents. It is important to make an effort whenever appropriate to ensure that important decisions are not made alone but shared with the significant people in our lives.

LIVE out our decision with courage, hope, and trust

This step requires us to trust in God and to decide, even in the absence of certitude. Sometimes fears and doubts can paralyze us and cause us to procrastinate in making important decisions. As Christians we are called to live boldly and decisively. We must act, even though our carefully discerned decisions may be tinged with some uncertainty due to variables beyond our control. We are called to trust in God's power at work bringing good out of everything. As Saint Paul says in Romans, "We know that all things work together for good for those who love God, who are called according to his purpose" (8:28).

It is also important to keep in mind that Ignatian consolation and desolation refer primarily to our relationship with God and should not be understood in terms of the pleasure-pain axis. Hence, a well-discerned choice can entail enduring periods of struggle and pain while at the same time be supported by a deep sense of God's presence and love.

Here we should also remember Ignatius's caveat about not making any significant decision when experiencing desolation (no. 318). For Ignatius, desolation is a time when we feel distant from God, confused and anxious. This time of darkness is not a good time to alter decisions that were freely made when in a state of consolation, a time when we experience an increase of faith, hope, love, and trust in God.

FRIEDRICH VON HUGEL'S THEORY OF INTEGRATED RELIGIOUS DEVELOPMENT

An understanding of religious development that supports a holistic approach to discernment can also be found in Friedrich von Hugel's two-volume work *The Mystical Element of Religion,* first published in 1908.[25] According to von Hugel, who was Evelyn Underhill's spiritual director, healthy spiritual growth includes three aspects of religion: the institutional, the critical, and the mystical. The institutional dimension of religion is of central importance in the early stages of personal development when children depend on sense impressions, memory, and instruction from others for their apprehension of religious belief. In the institutional stage of faith development, people believe because they have been taught by those whom they trust. They are the beneficiaries of a tradition, the recipients of the wisdom of a faith community. At this stage, "the External, Authoritative, Historical, Traditional, Institutional side and function of Religion are everywhere evident."[26]

The second stage, that of the critical, is a period of "trustful questioning, but still of questioning, first others, then oneself."[27] In this critical stage, which often characterizes adolescence, the human spirit's "reasoning, argumentative, abstractive side" demands recognition and "religion answers this demand by clear and systematic arguments and concatenations: this and this is now connected with that and that; this is true or this need not be false, because of that and that."[28] Finally, the third stage of religious development calls for the cultivation of an inner life and sensitivity to the world of interior experiences. "Here religion is rather felt than seen or reasoned about, is loved and lived rather than analyzed, is action and power, rather than either external fact or intellectual verification."[29]

According to von Hugel, there are clear historical examples of these three aspects of religion. In Judaism, "we find a severe and ardent external, traditional, authoritative school in the Pharisees; an accommodating and rationalizing school in the Sadducees; and...the experimental, ascetical, and mystical body of the Essenes."[30] Furthermore, he groups the New Testament writings according to the predominance of one of the three moods: the Petrine school illustrates the traditional, historic, external; the Pauline exemplifies the reasoning, speculative-internal; and the Johannine reflects the experimental, mystical-internal. Von Hugel concludes that ideal faith development in adults requires all three dimensions of religion:

> I believe because I am told, because it is true, because it answers to my deepest interior experiences and needs. And, everything else being equal, my faith will be at its richest and deepest and strongest, in so far as all three motives are most fully and characteristically operative within me, at one and the same time, and towards one and the same ultimate result and end.[31]

Von Hugel's understanding of integrative religious development lays the foundation for a holistic approach to discernment. Honoring the traditional guidance of one's faith community, his institutional stage validates the importance of a careful consideration of the wisdom of the group as handed on by tradition and taught by recognized authority. His stress on the importance of the critical dimension of religion affirms the necessity of adult reflection and questioning in the making of good decisions. Finally, von Hugel's mystical stage encourages Christians to value the data of their inner life and personal religious experience. The attractiveness of von Hugel's theory lies in its inclusiveness and balance. His stages are like sections of a tripartite bridge that help people journey through life. Each section must remain in place throughout the journey if the bridge is not to fall apart. Thus, he insists on the "joint presence" of the institutional, critical, and mystical aspects of religion, for "each of these three forces and elements is indeed necessary, but ruinously destructive where it more or less ousts the other two."[32]

When the institutional element predominates to the exclusion of the other two aspects, the result will be an infantilization of Christians and a loss of freedom; religion will then

> inevitably degenerate into more or less of a Superstition,—an oppressive materialization and dangerous would-be absolute fixation of even quite secondary and temporary expressions and analyses of religion; a ruinous belief in the direct transferableness of religious conviction; and a predominance of political, legal, physically coercive concepts and practices with regard to those most interior, strong yet delicate, readily thwarted or

weakened, springs of all moral and religious character,—spiritual sincerity and spontaneity and the lib-
erty of the children of God.[33]

Von Hugel's words, enunciated almost a century ago,
sound remarkably contemporary and aptly express the
feelings of the many people who fear the tyranny of the
institutional in today's church. He points to the Spanish
Inquisition as a clear example of the institutional element
gone awry in religion.

When the critical aspect is apotheosized, the results are
equally harmful. The worship of the god of reason leads
to a destructive one-sidedness, "a Rationalistic Fanaticism, only too often followed by a lengthy Agnosticism
and Indifference."[34] The critical element left alone is
liable to produce rationalists rather than religious persons, people whose devotion to an intellectual system
replaces their devotion to God. Those who foster the critical and neglect the other two elements are often suspicious of anything emotional and will tend to be out of
touch with the mystery of their own inner thoughts and
feelings, which are too complex to be captured in abstract
concepts. Frequently rigid and dogmatic, such people are
prone to be obsessed with the question of orthodoxy and
with exposing those whom they consider to be theologically unfaithful.

Finally, when the mystical dimension is cultivated at the
expense of the institutional and the critical, distortions
arise. In its worst form, the mystical element, unchecked
and cut off from the institutional and critical, can produce
dangerous fanaticism and extremism, as the example of Jim
Jones and the mass suicide of his cult followers clearly illustrate. Adrift from the critique of the community, the mystical element can isolate Christians and lead to the mindless

rejection of formal prayer and worship, the abandonment of doctrinal and moral teachings, and the growth of an emotionalism that cannot be understood because it refuses to submit itself to the critical element. When personal experience is canonized as the only legitimate source of discernment, the doors to anti-intellectualism and self-deception are left wide open.

USING VON HUGEL'S THEORY AS A DISCERNMENT TOOL

Von Hugel's three stages of integrated religious growth lend themselves easily to a simple, yet inclusive, approach to sorting through issues. When faced with a decision, for example, we can use his stages as a process guide.

- *In the institutional phase, we inquire whether our faith community or social group has any relevant data to offer regarding the issue.* This first step invites us to tap into the wisdom of a tradition-bearing community and thus benefit from the experiences and reflections of our predecessors. We might call this the hermeneutics of retrieval stage, in which we try to access our group's best thinking on the issue. To skip this step would be to deprive ourselves of possibly valuable input for our discernment.

    For mainline Christians today, this institutional aspect has been complicated by the existence of two very different ways of viewing the tradition. This difference has divided the contemporary church on such issues as the ordination of women, the union of gays and lesbians, and the path to salvation. Marcus Borg discusses these two competing views of being Christian. Labeling them as the "earlier" and the "emerging" paradigms, he concludes that "neither can claim to be *the* Christian tradition. Both are ways of seeing the tradition." These two ways of Christianity are so different, according to Borg, "that they almost produce two different religions, both using the same Bible and language."[35] Central to their radical difference is their understanding of biblical interpretation and the Bible's function in Christian life.

- *In the critical phase, we assess the data of tradition and the wisdom handed on by our community.* The teachings of tradition are important aspects of discernment because God's guidance can often be embodied in them. Of course, even tradition must be examined critically, with what theologians call a hermeneutic of suspicion, because the community too has made errors in the past from which much can be learned.

- *In the mystical phase, we pay close attention to the data of our own inner world of feelings, intuitions, gut-instincts, fantasies, desires, and aspirations.* As we sit with the various options before us, as well as the teachings of our community, we try to get a sense of which option best commands the agreement and consent of the whole self, resulting in the harmony of head, heart, and gut. The desired result is a decision that is based on a holistic knowing grounded in external authority, critical reasoning, and felt experience.

This method based on Von Hugel's theory is holistic because it allows us to blend outer authority with inner authority. A holistic discernment process encourages us to benefit from the wisdom of the community, which has accumulated a storehouse of insights about life's issues and problems based on shared experience. Dialoguing with others of common faith and values provides a healthy check on our internal process, opens us to feedback, and helps ensure that we do not slide down the slippery slope of self-deception. However, discernment falters if it does not include paying serious attention to our inner life and honoring our inner authority. This prayerful attention to how God might be leading us through our thoughts and feelings, fantasies and desires, dreams and drives, bodily sensations and intuitions is what Christian spirituality refers to as solitude of heart. Solitude of heart entails cultivating a quiet inner center, a receptive space, where we can tune in to our inner voices and the voice of God within. Holistic discernment encourages us to befriend our inner life because it is a source of self-knowledge and a storehouse of personal wisdom.

Working with Our Inner Wisdom Circle

As a practical way of deepening an awareness of God's voice speaking within, it is helpful to imagine an inner wisdom circle in which a meeting of the various parts of the self is taking place. Of course, each person's inner circle has a personal configuration. Holistic discernment requires us to pay careful attention to the dynamics of our inner deliberation.

- Are all the legitimate representatives of the self given a respected place and a fair say in the meeting? Which parts are typically left out and need to be invited to participate?
- Which part(s) typically exercises power and control?
- Which part(s) typically experiences difficulty in being heard and respected?
- Is any part given to monopolizing and dominating the conversation?
- How is the guidance of divine Wisdom typically made known in our inner wisdom circle?

In this inner dialogue or conversation among the various aspects of the self, it is important that each part of the plural self feels that it has had its say and has been understood. It is also important that no one part monopolizes the discussion and tries to force its way on the self.

In a culture that worships reason and the scientific, objective mind, for example, it is critical to remember that, in the words of psychologist Carl Rogers, people are wiser than their intellects. When we face a decision, we might ask ourselves whether our feelings are being taken into account? Or do we say to ourselves: "Let's be objective; stick to the facts and keep feelings out of this!" Women's liberation has also happily liberated men. When feelings and hunches were once denigrated as merely women's intuition—not a solid basis for making decisions—everyone lost a potentially important resource. Ignoring feelings simply makes them go underground and operate outside of reasonable control, undermining the decisions in which they were given no say. On the other hand, we need to ask ourselves whether or not we allow our feelings to drown out the other voices in that inner wisdom circle. Either case—refusing to give feelings their say or letting feelings dominate—makes for poor discernment. The proper function of reflection is not the suppression of spontaneity, wants, and feelings, but rather the liberation of wants and feelings from impulsive reactions to immediate stimuli.

III.
SPIRIT-LED IN MANY WAYS

The wind blows where it chooses, and you hear the sound of it,
but you do not know where it comes from or where it goes.
So it is with everyone who is born of the Spirit.

—John 3:8

THE HEART OF DISCERNMENT is being in tune with the Spirit
of God in our choices and actions. This core notion of discernment stems from the earliest understanding in Christianity about what constitutes the spiritual person. In the
letters of Paul, the spiritual person is viewed as one who is
sensitive and docile to the promptings of the Spirit in the
ordinary context of life. Paul called such people "spiritual"
or *pneumatikos,* a word he coined from the Greek word
pneuma, meaning "spirit."[1] This Pauline understanding
squares solidly with what is amply illustrated in the Gospel
of Luke and the Acts of the Apostles. For Luke, the Holy
Spirit is the gift par excellence that God bestows on believers (Luke 11:13). The Spirit fills and animates holy people
like Elizabeth and Zechariah, the parents of John the Baptist (Luke 1:41, 67), and sways the Baptizer's own life "even
before his birth" (Luke 1:15). Jesus is conceived through the
power of the Holy Spirit (Luke 1:35) and is himself filled
with the Spirit, who leads him into the desert (Luke 4:1). In
Acts, the Spirit's activity remains prominent: the Spirit

empowers the disciples to preach the gospel (Acts 2:1–17), guides the emerging church in expanding its mission (15:28), and directs the missionaries on their journeys (16:6–7). Acts illustrates how God relies on the disciples to embody the real, though imperceptible, presence of the risen Jesus. The Spirit of Jesus is given flesh and blood reality in the lives of his disciples: in Peter, who cures the paralytic at the Temple gate called Beautiful (3:1–10), and in Stephen, who prays that those putting him to death will be forgiven (7:60). Peter's cure of the lame beggar and Stephen's prayer of forgiveness both trigger vivid memories of Jesus' own words and actions. In this way they convey the Lukan theme that the Spirit of Jesus continues to be active in history—but now embodied in the lives of his disciples. In short, faithful followers of Jesus are those who are led by the Spirit.

A WIDE VIEW OF HOW SPIRIT LEADS

In her research on spiritual discernment, psychotherapist and spiritual director Nancy Reeves narrates the discernment stories of seventy-eight people (fifty-seven based on her own interviews and the rest taken from published works). Based on what she discovered in her survey of the discernment practices of a broad range of believers of various faith traditions, she argues for the need to approach discernment with "a wider vision" of the diverse ways our lives can be influenced by God:

> Some of the discernment methods presented here will remind you of your own graced history. Others may intrigue you or invite you to sample them. A few may seem so foreign or weird that it seems unimaginable

how they could be valid. But an infinite God can contact us in unlimited ways.[2]

A sampling of what Reeves discovered in her study concretely illustrates her conclusion that God leads people with different strings of love.

In the story of Tanya, Reeves illustrates how someone was led to honor the wisdom of her body, more specifically, her sexual energy. Tanya started off by saying that God speaks to her in many ways such as devotional reading, other people, dreams, and so on. Then she went on to describe an intense religious experience that revealed to her a new way of detecting God's lead. At a time in her life when she was not feeling her sexuality very strongly, she woke up around 3:30 in the morning feeling surprisingly intense sexual arousal. Finding this experience strange and disturbing, she initially suspected that her body was acting up to expose how unspiritual she really was. But when she took these uncomfortable feelings to prayer with the hope of receiving some divine illumination, she found an astonishing thing: "The more receptive to God I became, the stronger the sexual feelings grew." With her image of herself as a spiritual being above all "animal urges" threatened, she felt miserable, though strangely her body "was zinging with life and energy." The sexual sensations continued through the morning. She was embarrassed about feeling so sexual and felt ambivalent about keeping her afternoon spiritual-direction appointment. She wondered to herself how her spiritual director, a celibate nun, could provide any help. In the end, she kept her appointment, thinking that perhaps Sister Jo might be the best person to talk to after all, since she must have had experience of getting rid of sexual feelings:

When Sister Jo and I met, I looked at her welcoming
face and felt my own face turning red. How could I
start? I said, "God is very creative." She nodded and
waited. "I mean, really, creative." She waited. "And,
um, very, kind of, sexual." "Ah," she responded quite
matter of factly. "Are you having experiences of making love to Jesus?" "Oh no!" I replied with horror.
(Pause) "It feels like the Holy Spirit. And we're not
making love. I just feel this intense sexuality and the
more I open to God, the stronger it gets."

Following an explanation of how the mystical tradition of
Christianity tells of men and women having similar experiences, Sister Jo encouraged Tanya to be open to enjoying
God in this way. Even with her spiritual director's support,
it took Tanya months "to become easy with this aspect of
Holy Mystery." Reflecting on what she has learned about
discernment, Tanya comments:

My body is often more truthful about a need than my
mind is. I saw how I was judging my body. I thought
the way to God was through my heart and mind....
Then I realized that God wanted me to use this sexual
energy for discernment....When I ask for direction,
and hold various choices in my heart and mind, there
will often be more sexual energy around one of them.

Reeves concludes the story of Tanya by citing psychiatrist
and spiritual director Gerald May, who says in his *The Awak-
ened Heart,* "Sometimes [God's Love] is felt and expressed
in ways that are undeniably sexual: yearning, embracing,
excitement, fulfillment, and resting so deep and physical
that one can never again doubt the fullness of divine incar-
nation."[3]

In relating the story of Adele, Reeves illustrates how physical disability has gracefully introduced a new way for Adele

to experience God's lead. When driving on a mountain road, Adele had a car accident that has permanently changed her life. She was unconscious for some time, and she suffered extensive physical damage. While newly invented surgical procedures saved her life and partially restored her ability to walk, the head injury she sustained greatly affected her mental capacity. She experiences extreme fatigue and struggles with concentration, abstract thinking, short-term memory, and understanding in general:

> Before the accident, if I wasn't sure whether the Lord wanted me to go with "A" or "B," I would hold each in my mind and wait to see which was accompanied by a feeling of deep peace and "rightness." That's the one I'd go with. Now I can't keep the thoughts in mind long enough to get an answer. I often forget what the question is.

Faced with the reality of her impaired state, Adele "wondered how I would know God's will since the old discernment way did not work." A woman of deep faith, she was grateful to discover a new personal way of discerning:

> One day, to help me remember, I held out my hands, palm up, and said, "Lord, 'A' is in my right hand and 'B' is in my left. Which do you want me to do?" And you know what? One hand heated up! It is so clear which way to go. I do that frequently now. Sometimes the answer comes immediately and sometimes I have to wait for awhile. For me, now, it has to be clear and concrete.[4]

Two more stories related by Reeves serve well to stretch our understanding of the multiplicity of ways in which individuals experience God's guidance. At a discernment workshop conducted by Dr. Reeves, a woman named Candace spoke of a time when she was "sunk deep" in contemplative prayer:

> Candace experienced a "rich, refreshing" taste in her mouth. This taste recurred quite frequently, at first in prayer and then during her daily life. She knew this taste was of God. One day, she was trying to decide between two options that seemed equally appealing and beneficial to her. As she thought of one, she experienced the taste. When she thought of the other, it disappeared. Candace took this as a sign to start down the first path.

In a similar way a woman named Laura shared how she felt God's guidance through her physical sensations:

> Since I was a little child, I have had a physical sensation of the Holy. God speaks to me in a combination of sensation and awareness. I know the path God wants me to take when I experience a marvelous enlivening feeling that makes my body seem larger. Frequently, there is an electric current that starts at my feet and radiates through my body. This is accompanied by an awareness that I feel in my heart. This discernment is most common for me in nature.

Long accustomed to finding God's guidance through traditional church structures and activities, Laura felt a shift:

> I felt the divine calling to me in every place *but* the church. I was being called out and away. But called to what?...Increasingly, I was aware of the sacredness of the beach, of all creation. Experiencing God potently in everything and every moment. I realized that I had been focused too much on God in formalized worship within a particular building.[5]

Reeves's research findings verify what spiritual teachers have long intuited: life is laced with grace, and we need to be open in diverse ways to the mysterious epiphanies of God everywhere. "Most of the people I interviewed," states Reeves, "stressed that their story of discernment was only *one* way that they were called to understand God's will for them. As they became more aware of their constant, 'hands-on' relationship with the All, they found guidance occurring more often and in many different ways."[6] God attracts some people through the beauty of nature or the wonders of creation. Others feel the allurement of God in the emotional stirrings of their hearts or the penetrating insights of their minds. Music, mandalas, physical movement, and stillness are yet other ways that heighten people's sensitivity to God's ineffable presence.

THE THEORY OF MULTIPLE INTELLIGENCES

When we speak of God's immanence, we acknowledge that the Spirit of God pervades the whole universe and can direct our choices through the ordinary human ways that we come to know. Psychologist Howard Gardner has proposed an understanding of human intelligence that provides some cognitive basis for the wide variety of ways that Reeves's interviewees report discerning the direction of the Spirit in their lives. According to Gardner, all human beings are smart in at least seven different ways:

> Multiple intelligence theory posits a small set of human intellectual potentials, perhaps as few as seven in number, of which all individuals are capable by virtue of their membership in the human species. Owing to heredity, early training, or, in all probability, a constant interaction between these factors, some

individuals will develop certain intelligences far more than others; but every normal individual should develop each intelligence to some extent, given but a modest opportunity to do so.[7]

Viewed theologically, Gardner's theory tells us that human beings are gifted by the Creator with at least seven different ways of knowing.

Challenging our ingrained views that make intelligence synonymous with linguistically mediated thought, Gardner lists the following seven different types of intelligence:

1. Linguistic
2. Logical-mathematical
3. Bodily-kinesthetic
4. Spatial
5. Musical
6. Interpersonal
7. Intra-personal

In general, the standardized tests we administer to measure intelligence and aptitude for college and postgraduate studies mainly test for verbal and math skills. These measurements only reflect linguistic and logical-mathematical intelligence. One might assume from these tests that human intelligence is reducible to those two ways of knowing. Gardner challenges this long-held assumption and calls us to reclaim and revalue the many other ways that human beings can be smart. People who are more bodily-kinesthetically oriented in their learning, for example, process knowledge through bodily sensation. Those who are spatial learners think in images and pictures. Music-oriented learners possess a keen awareness of sounds and are often discriminating listeners. Interpersonal learners are sharply aware of their emotional environment and read people's feelings and intentions well. Intra-personal learners possess a keen facility to monitor their inner life.

In a technological society that so often equates intelligence with analytic and linguistic competence, we tend not to recognize that people are smart in many other ways. Martha Graham, the famous modern dancer, once observed: "I have often remarked on the extreme difficulty of having any kind of conversation with most dancers which has any kind of logical cohesiveness—their minds just jump around (maybe like my body)—the logic—such as it is—occurs on the level of motor activity."[8] Nevertheless, the intelligence of superb dancers is undeniable when we consider how executing a dance movement precisely entails complex skills regarding placement, stage spacing, the quality of a leap, and the softness of the foot.

Actors, too, exhibit intelligence in their ability to observe carefully and then to re-create scenes in detail. Acting teacher Richard Boleslavsky highlights the peculiar intelligence required of actors when he says: "The gift of observation must be cultivated in every part of your body, not only in your sight and memory....Everything registers anatomically somewhere in my brain and through the practice of recalling and reenacting, I am ten times as alert as I was."[9] The kind of intelligence possessed by athletes often goes unappreciated when their excellent performance is casually attributed to bodily endowment alone. Yet, many intellectual strengths contribute to the success of talented athletes, such as the logical ability to devise a good strategy, the ability to recognize familiar spatial patterns and to exploit them on the spot, and an interpersonal perceptiveness about the personalities and intentions of other players in the game.[10]

Interpersonal and intra-personal intelligences are often given short shrift in our society. Yet these intellectual competences are critical to satisfying relationships and personal well-being. As described by Gardner, people's interpersonal intelligence enables them to read the intentions and desires—even hidden ones—of others and to act upon this knowledge. Religious and political leaders, skilled parents, teachers, and helping professionals commonly possess a high degree of interpersonal intelligence. Intra-personal or intra-psychic intelligence allows people to have access to their own feeling life with its range of affects or emotions. Intra-personally intelligent people are able to discriminate among their feelings, name them, and communicate them. This form of intelligence is evident in people such as writers, who can write introspectively about feelings; actors, who can access the feelings and emotions a role demands; and wise mentors, who can tap into their own rich reservoir of inner experiences to guide others.

MULTIPLE INTELLIGENCES AND DISCERNMENT

Not surprisingly, Gardner's theory of multiple intelligences has led some educational reformers to devise pedagogical methods aimed at playing to each student's strength or natural way of processing, and thus enhance learning. "In my view," argues Gardner, "it should be possible to identify an individual's intellectual profile (or proclivities) at an early age and then draw upon this knowledge to enhance that person's educational opportunities and options."[11] When applied to the process of spiritual development and discernment skills, Gardner's idea of multiple intelligences encourages us to recognize and foster people's personal, and often idiosyncratic, ways of connecting with God and divine guidance. Analogous to its application to educational reform, multiple-intelligence theory applied to spiritual formation calls us to respect the personal and unique ways each of us detects the presence and influence of God. We need to take seriously our own spiritual profile or proclivities, that is, our natural "bent" in knowing spiritually what God wants of us. By doing so, we can strengthen our proficiency in discerning.

WISDOM OF THE BODY

Gardner's kinesthetic-bodily intelligence is perhaps another way of speaking about what is commonly referred to as the "wisdom of the body." In his book *Focusing*, Eugene Gendlin introduced a technique for "unlocking the wisdom of the body" by focusing on a kind of bodily awareness he calls "felt sense." A felt sense is a physical experience, not a mental one, according to Gendlin. It is "a bodily awareness of a situation or person or event. An internal aura that encompasses everything you feel and know about the given subject at a given time—encompassing it and communicating it to you all at once rather than detail by detail."[12] Gendlin's felt sense is similar to what is popularly referred to as intuition, an inner grasp or insight into the nature of some reality without detailed analysis. Some of the people interviewed by Reeves come to mind (for example, Adele, Candace, and Laura), when Gendlin further describes a felt sense as "a kind of taste, if you like, or a great musical chord that makes you feel a powerful impact, a big round unclear feeling. A felt sense doesn't come to you in the form of thoughts or words or other separate units, but as a single (though often puzzling and very complex) bodily feeling."[13] Sometimes used in spiritual direction, the focusing skill developed by Gendlin is a way of accessing the intelligence stored in the body. "The body is like a biological computer," he states, "generating these enormous collections of data and delivering them to you instantaneously when you call them up or when they are called up by some external event."[14]

For Gendlin and others the body is viewed as an indwelling intelligence with its own remarkable sense of rightness and acute feeling for enlivening solutions. Gestalt therapy, for example, views bodily expressions as "truth buttons" that reveal the intrinsic wisdom of the organism. That is why Gestalt therapists make body awareness a central focus in their work with clients. In their clinical practice these therapists regularly take note of perceived discrepancies between their patients' verbal language and their body language. They ask:

> Are they the same voice? Is the message unified? Or is there a split between what the person says with his mouth and what he says with the rest of himself? This splitting, when it is present, is a factor in the total crisis situation; and if the person fails to understand what the many levels of the organism express, he may remain the proverbial house divided—he fails to make peace with himself.[15]

Gestalt therapists aim to expand awareness so that their clients can become more "response-able," that is, able to make life-giving choices in the concrete circumstances of their lives. Their focus on body awareness stems from the belief that our body often reveals what our words conceal. One way of expanding awareness is by breaking down various forms of conditioned behavior, sometimes called hypnotic states or, according to Fritz Perls, "the state of dreaming." One form of these hypnotic states, Vincent F. O'Connell writes, is the "hypnosis of the spoken word":

This conditioned behavior is present when the person fails to realize that his verbal language may not be empirical fact, but mere verbalism....The person creates for himself a "verbal world," which is to say a world of words and sounds in which the musical note of the organism is heard faintly, or not at all. When that is one of his hypnotic states, we need to jog his other senses, even to force him sometimes to be silent so that he can begin to hear once again the more central note of the organism.[16]

A personal experience illustrates well how the body can quickly point out a liberating truth that the mind was for months reluctant to accept. In 1972, a year before completing my doctoral work at the University of California, Santa Barbara, I agreed to my Jesuit superior's plan to assign me to Bellarmine College Preparatory in San Jose to serve as an assistant principal for curriculum and faculty development. Though my superior offered other options, I thought that working to bring about creative educational changes at Bellarmine was what I wanted to do and should do. About six months before the date scheduled for my official arrival, I visited the school, met the faculty, and saw my new office. During the course of that day of orientation, I noticed that my back got increasingly tight; by mid-afternoon it was in a painful knot. My aching back signaled a problem and led eventually to my "backing out." This sudden turn of events came as a big surprise, not only to those who counted on me, but also to me, because I had, until then, a reputation for being steady and dependable.

Months of previous conversations and correspondence contained no hint that going to Bellarmine would be problematic for me. It was my aching back that finally forced me to face the truth that I did not want a career in secondary school administration. Clearly, my verbal language and body language were saying different things! Reflecting on what led to such a flawed discernment, I was able to identify two factors: one, an unconscious guilt stemming from my enjoyment of doctoral studies in the luxurious surroundings of Santa Barbara, while five of my newly ordained Jesuit classmates toiled tirelessly in our high school two hours away in the inner city of Los Angeles; two, my unconscious tendency to please authority figures. In retrospect, that painful and embarrassing no was graceful in that it freed me to say yes to a more life-giving ministry in the spiritual formation of Jesuits and yes to an emerging self that was autonomous enough to withstand the disapproval of others.

LETTING THE BODY CHOOSE

Sometimes the mind can so entangle us in analyzing options that long periods of deliberation can muddle rather than clarify our choice. A sophistic chorus of inner voices seems to argue effectively for each of the alternatives before us. At such times, calling for clarification from the body can be beneficial. A technique used both in spiritual direction and psychotherapy entails letting our body choose. It is often used after months, possibly years, of talking that has not led to a clear choice. The process is quite simple: First, clients are asked to visualize different points in the office as representing each of the options that are under consideration. For example, the door might represent option A; the desk, option B; and the floor lamp, option C. Clients are then given ten seconds to choose by walking to the place representing their final decision. No matter what they do, the results are always illuminating. For example, some people will immediately bolt out of the chair and walk directly, without hesitation, to the place representing their preference. They surprise themselves by knowing exactly what they want, even though their words have consistently expressed confusion and ambivalence. Others might find themselves, by the end of the count, pulled, for example, between options A and C. While no definitive answer has come to them, the exercise has narrowed the focus of discernment by eliminating option B. If, as sometimes happens, clients find themselves paralyzed and unable to get out of the chair, we know that an impasse has been reached and further work is necessary to uncover its meaning.

While famous philosophers and writers such as Friedrich Wilhelm Nietzsche and D. H. Lawrence have acclaimed bodily wisdom, it is also common to hear testimonials to the wisdom of the body in ordinary life. A spiritual directee in the midst of discerning whether to take on a new position of responsibility, for example, said:

> In my body, my experience of this yes was very different than other times in my life. I had a keen awareness during the final days of this discernment of my body's energy. I could recognize with certainty where I felt positive energy, and where the energy felt depleted or absent. I became confident that my experience of that vitality was what would lead me to my best decision. I decided I would not say yes unless I felt it.

Another example of reliance on bodily wisdom comes from a graduate student reflecting on a recent decision regarding purchasing a home. His account makes clear how awareness of his body guided him in the process:

> After we placed an offer on the home we thought we wanted, I experienced a sick feeling in my stomach— especially in the mornings—that made it difficult for me even to eat. I am familiar with this sick feeling in

my stomach. I experience it when I am dealing with something difficult or stressful. I also experienced a lack of creativity and a preoccupied mind during the time when we were waiting to see if the offer on this home would be accepted or rejected. When my wife and I decided to remove our offer on the above mentioned home and place an offer on a different home, the discomfort in my stomach went away immediately. Also, my creativity returned immediately. I was able to accomplish in a five-hour afternoon the work I had been trying to do continuously for one week with no results. It appears that I was feeling desolation about the first home and consolation about the second home.

These examples are popularly referred to as gut feelings. Based on their own past experiences, many people have come to trust the reliability of these gut feelings in guiding their discernment.

GUT FEELINGS AND THE BRAIN

The work of Antonio Damasio, M.D., professor of neurology at the University of Iowa School of Medicine, has suggested a clear neurological explanation of the nature of our gut feelings. In his book *Descartes' Error,* Damasio shows how bodily states and emotions are indispensable to our rational decision-making process. He builds his theory around the idea of somatic or bodily markers, which are like marked cards buried in a deck. These markers take the shape of bodily responses such as our gut tightening in fear, our back knotting up in anxiety, or our chest warming in contentment. Events that trigger such intense bodily reactions are encoded in positive or negative memories that affect our intuitive responses to everyday situations, though they are largely subliminal. When confronting decisions, the emotional brain flags specific options as desirable or repulsive based on information retained in the brain from past emotional experiences. By doing so, it enables us to narrow down the possible options in any given situation. In other words, bodily states and emotions become associated with certain outcomes and thus influence our decisions. In this way somatic markers steer us toward a certain decision.

Damasio first recognized the importance of emotion in decision-making when working with patients whose emotional centers had been damaged by strokes, accidents, or tumors. For example, patients with frontal lobe damage failed to generate the normal skin conductance responses in reacting to emotional slides.[17] According to Damasio, "All these people shared one common trait: their emotions were compromised....They were flattened, compared to the way they used to be, and compared to what we normally expect from people. Social emotions—shame, embarrassment—were specifically compromised."[18] Damasio suspected that his patients' inability to be emotional was getting in the way of their reasoning. Despite their intact intelligence, these patients made disastrous personal and professional decisions. They obsessed endlessly over simple everyday decisions because they had lost access to their emotional learning, those emotional likes and dislikes acquired over the course of one's experience and stored in the brain's memory; "the patients were not making use of the emotion-related experience they had accumulated in their lifetime."[19] Damasio states:

> Decisions made in these emotion-impoverished circumstances led to erratic or downright negative results, especially so in terms of future consequences....Choosing a career, deciding whether to

> marry, or launching a new business are examples of
> decisions whose outcomes are uncertain, regardless of
> how carefully prepared one may be when the decision
> is made. Typically one has to choose among conflict-
> ing options, and emotions and feelings come in handy
> in those circumstances.[20]

In other words, instinctual emotional responses support efficient rational choice. Without these gut feelings, patients were prone to get caught up in endless cycles of analysis, mentally weighing infinite lists of pros and cons. "It's not that I'm saying the emotions decide things *for* you. It's that the emotions help you concentrate on the right decision."[21] For Damasio, our gut feelings do not substitute for proper reasoning but have an important auxiliary function that increases "the efficiency of the reasoning process" and makes it speedier. "On occasion," he states, "it may make the reasoning process almost superfluous, such as when we immediately reject an option that would lead to certain disaster, or, on the contrary, we jump to a good opportunity based on a high probability of success."[22]

THE IMAGINATION AND DISCERNMENT

Besides affirming the value of kinesthetic-bodily intelligence, the notion of multiple intelligences invites us to value the importance and usefulness of the imagination in discernment. "There is no life of the spirit without imagination," state Ann and Barry Ulanov, "yet people constantly belittle or trivialize it....Properly understood and pursued, the imagination is perhaps our most reliable way of bringing the world of the unconscious into some degree of consciousness and our best means of corresponding with the graces offered us in the life of the spirit."[23] Written in the

early 1920s, Bernard Shaw's play *Saint Joan* captures how
the imagination as a source of useful knowledge has long
been regarded with suspicion:

Robert: What did you mean when you said that St.
Catherine and St. Margaret talked to you every
day?

Joan: They do.

Robert: What are they like?

Joan: (suddenly obstinate) I will tell nothing about
that; they have not given me leave.

Robert: But you actually see them; and they talk to you
just as I am talking to you?

Joan: No; it is quite different. I cannot tell you: you
must not talk to me about my voices.

Robert: How do you mean voices?

Joan: I hear voices telling me what to do. They come
from God.

Robert: They come from your imagination.

Joan: Of course. That is how the messages of God
come to us.[24]

While most people readily agree that the imagination contributes richly to the arts, its possible contribution to the
weightier matters of human affairs is generally discounted.
American society has seemingly exiled the imagination to
Disneyland and Hollywood and excluded its role in the serious business of decision-making in the real world.

The imagination has long been undervalued in decision-
making. As children growing up, we often heard our parents and teachers telling us how important it is to "think
ahead" when making decisions. While reason and foresight
are valuable ways of anticipating possible consequences of
our choices, the use of reason is only one means. Besides

reason, imagination has a great part to play in foreseeing the consequences of actions, and imagination can powerfully support reason in the process. Visualizing how various courses of action might end up is much more useful than merely thinking abstractly about it. Thinking only involves our head. Fantasizing, as a serious exercise in awareness, calls for inserting our whole self into a situation. By doing this, we can actually *experience ahead of time* the possible consequences of an act. For example, when considering the question of whether or not to have a certain kind of surgery done, it is important not only to *think* about the biological, sexual, and interpersonal consequences that such an operation might have, but also to anticipate, in a "head, heart, and gut" way, what subjective responses these consequences might evoke in us and in others. What effect would such an act have on our feelings and sense of self? Through the imagination we can live out, in fantasy, the various consequences of choice.

If the imagination can be helpful in discernment, we might ask ourselves whether our fantasies, daydreams, and nocturnal dreams are given a voice in our inner wisdom circle. In his autobiography Ignatius of Loyola recounts how he was able to discern God's will for his life by paying careful attention to his daydreams. He discovered that after daydreams of doing chivalrous deeds for a noble lady whose love he would win, he felt excited, hopeful, and uplifted. Then, when dreaming of imitating such saints as Saint Francis and Saint Dominic in selflessly serving God, he felt similarly inspired, motivated, and uplifted. But after a while, he noticed a psychic shift occurring. The positive feelings that once encircled his secular fantasy of knightly gallantry evaporated like dry ice, but the positive feelings surrounding his saintly ambitions remained strong and compelling. Dreaming of outdoing the saints ultimately fueled his conversion and energized his new life of service to God. By engaging his imagination and attending to the affective aftermath of his fantasies, he acquired his first lesson in what he was later to call discernment of spirits. Similarly, when struggling with choices, we might look at our own daydreams and ask how we feel at the end of them. Are we bored and empty, or hopeful and encouraged? Noticing the affective aftermath of our daydreams is a way of letting our fantasy life provide its wisdom, as it did for Ignatius. Ignatius's suggestion that the imagination can support reasoning in the discernment process is not unlike Damasio's argument that emotions provide important support to reasoning in decision-making.

IMAGINATION AND HOPEFUL ACTION

When an attitude of "that's the way things are" dominates our consciousness, we can find ourselves stuck in painful and unsatisfying situations. Apathy results from feeling that nothing in our situation can be changed and that we have no choice but to bear with our sufferings. Unable to conceive of how things can be other than they are, an impoverished imagination leaves us stranded and stuck. Only a lively imagination can lift us from such paralysis by suggesting how things can be different. French existentialist philosopher Jean-Paul Sartre highlights the important role of the imagination in fighting off apathy and fueling meaningful action for bettering our lives. "It is on the day that we can conceive of a different state of affairs," he states, "that a new light falls on our troubles and our suffering and that we *decide* that these are unbearable."[25] Our sufferings in themselves, according to Sartre, cannot motivate us to act. It is only when we realize, with the help of the imagination, that our sufferings are not inevitable, that things could be otherwise, that a dramatic shift in consciousness occurs: the suffering that we once thought to be bearable now becomes unbearable. Unbearable suffering supplies the commitment and motive for change.

In what he calls "a double nihilation," Sartre delineates the process involved in this call to action instigated by the imagination. The first nihilation entails recognizing the fact that the "ideal state of affairs" that our imagination has suggested exists only "as a pure *present* nothingness." In other words, at this stage it only exists in our imagination, not in the real world. The second nihilation involves juxtaposing our actual situation with the desired change envisioned and acknowledging "the actual situation as nothingness in relation to the ideal." In short, we can break through our apathetic resignation to bad situations only when we employ our imagination to help us envision how things can be other than they are. When we value the possibilities that we perceive and then convert our perceptions into personal projects for change, we can engage in discernment with a lively spirit of hope. Sartre's process illustrates well how the imagination can restore juice to a dehydrated discernment process resulting from excessive doses of "that's the way things are."

DISCERNMENT AS UNIQUELY PERSONAL

Discernment is not formulaic; it is more like an individual art that we must develop through learning and experience. God's mysterious guidance comes to us in personal and unique ways that we must honor. We need to be aware of the idiosyncratic ways in which we are influenced and led by the Divine, as well as the personal ways we are susceptible to being deceived and misled. In discernment, there is no general "best" path for everyone; each of us must discover—by prayerfully reflecting on our concrete experience of life—the path intended for us. Spiritual guides must also respect the unique ways by which God leads various individuals. In other words, they must watch for the error of thinking of discernment as a monolithic process, uniform and same for all.

On the positive side, we need to value the peculiar ways we find ourselves responsive to the mystery of God's presence. So, when discerning, it is important to know from past experience how God has uniquely dealt with us and to honor our individual religious sensibility. Past experience can be a valuable guide. Reflect, for example, on the following:

- In the past, when you got it right, when you "knew that you knew" how God was leading you, and subsequent experience confirmed the rightness of your discernment, what did you do? What process or approach did you follow? How would you describe the nuances and qualities of that experience?
- When evaluating any new situation or choice, you can use your past periods of spiritual consolation as a touchstone. Visualize those graceful periods when you experienced closeness to God and inner harmony, peace, and joy, as a deep well. Drop your present preference or choice into that well as you might drop a coin. If the sound you hear when the coin (your present decision) hits the bottom is harmonious and peaceful, there is a rightness or harmony between it and how you have experienced God's consoling presence in the past. If the sound you hear is jarring and discordant, your present decision is not in harmony with the way God operates in your life. What is being checked out is whether or not the new decision is congruent with past

states of consolation.[26] This method reflects the belief
that "spiritual discernment proceeds less by way of
rational analysis than by affective consonance or dissonance. One interprets the affective resonances of a
given experience. The discerner 'senses' what is in
accord with or in opposition to God's will. The judgment is by a 'feel' for the truth. It is judging by connat-
urality or affinity, much as a chaste person, for
example, knows intuitively what is or is not chaste in a
given case."[27]

• Or recall a concrete peak religious experience or
event when you intensely and palpably felt God's loving presence. What was that peak experience of consolation like? What did you feel? What did you think?
What bodily sensations did you have? When you "dip"
your present experience while discerning into that
touchstone experience, do you experience resonance
or dissonance? A feeling of resonance is affective reassurance that you are in touch with God's presence; a
feeling of dissonance indicates that your present
choice does not harmonize with what you experience
when you are in touch with God.

LEARNING FROM OUR MISTAKES

On the negative side, reflection on past mistakes can also
teach us about tendencies that can lead to a flawed discernment process. An experiential approach to discernment
allows for trial-and-error learning and leaves room for mistakes. Ignatius, considered in the Christian tradition as a
master of discernment, is often quoted as saying that he
learned how not to make mistakes by making many. Or, as a
contemporary spiritual writer puts it: "Nothing in the

whole gamut of my life experience needs to be wasted. Everything and everyone can teach me something;...nothing is wasted unless I refuse to 'gather' it, refuse to let it in....And most of those potential wastes can be avoided by the simple practice of attentiveness."[28] Learning from experience requires pondering such questions as these:

- In the past, when you got it wrong, when you somehow were misled, what steered you off the track? Are there particular vulnerabilities or tendencies you have to guard against when making decisions?
- Do you rely exclusively on your reasoning without paying attention to the data provided by your body and your feelings? Or do you let feelings blindly hold sway without benefiting from rational analysis?
- Do you tend to rush into important decisions without giving yourself enough time for prayerful reflection? Or do you tend to procrastinate or delay important decisions unnecessarily?
- Do you tend to rely on others too much and not pay sufficient attention to what is going on in your inner life and trust your own inner wisdom? Or do you tend to finalize important decisions without sufficient consultation?
- Does a tendency to please others result in your denying your own needs? Do the "shoulds" of others take priority over your own desires?
- Does human respect or a desire to be seen or regarded in a certain way prevent you from doing what you feel called by God to do?
- Does an excessive need for others' approval or an excessive sense of responsibility for others impede your ability to make life-giving choices?

- Does an inordinate attachment to someone or something block you from choosing freely?

Being reflective about our personal experiences and tendencies makes sound discernment possible. The following account of a spiritual directee vividly illustrates the importance of knowing our personal pitfalls and being open to the help of grace:

> When discerning, I am always so concerned with what others want, with pleasing others. I have often felt anxious when standing up for what I want or what I need. I have been too concerned with fear of taking a risk and asking for what I need only to be told no, to have a situation where I have no power, where I take a risk and lose everything. I also have feelings of guilt that what I want or need will make others unhappy or interfere with their lives. Whose needs come first? Why is it that what I feel I need or am being drawn to is always different from what others want or see for me? Why is it that it is so often in conflict with the desires of those around me? When is it being selfish and when is it right to follow this kind of path?
>
> Well, there is enough fear, what ifs, and second guessing going on in my head to last a lifetime right now. I think God wants me to "go with the flow," but I just can't seem to figure out how to do it. It is tough to transition from being a people pleaser to being an authentic person. I can't do this on my own. I feel an intense rush of emotion as I face this reality. I know that God will give me the grace to do it.
>
> I am ready to let go of my fears and concerns about what others want and think...and to be honest about what I need and where I believe I will be able to best serve. I am scared, but I am ready to move beyond the fear. Something clicked last week. Hearing a friend

share about trusting her inner wisdom really touched me. Just that morning I had tried to quiet my own inner voice once again as one of my superiors tried to convince me that I was needed as the vice principal. I know that these people are good and wise. I also know that they care about me and respect me. That is why it is so hard to trust my own voice over what they say. But I am ready to trust what I have felt in my heart, what I know in my head, and what I have been shown in my prayer. It is time for me to be real. I trust in you, Lord, help my lack of trust.

SOUND DISCERNMENT IS REALITY BASED

Spiritual writer Pierre Wolff elaborates helpfully on the importance of making sure our decisions are grounded in the real world of what is. Reality-based choices entail

- [taking] myself as I am and not as I dream of being: [accepting] my body (my size, my face, my man- or womanhood, my health); my mind (sharp, slow, intelligent, imaginative); my sense of organization; my capacity to perceive what is important, my tendency to get lost in details; my heart (sensitive, vulnerable, shy, guarded, loving, compassionate, afraid); my heredity, education, training, past experiences, values; [being] the one I am without a mask or without trying to play a role—objectively and realistically [being] the one I am.
- [taking] others as they are and not as I would like them to be...where they are now instead of where I want them to be; their ideas, opinions, reactions, past, culture, aspirations, dreams.
- [taking] facts as they are: [looking] at the real situation as it is, without prejudices and, if possible, unemotionally, with objectivity.

- [accepting] the "here and now"; this place, this time, and not elsewhere; [accepting] the ambiguities of human life with its ups and downs, never perfectly black or white;...[seeing] what is possible right now.[29]

CONCLUSION

James and Evelyn Whitehead have provided a description of the "wise woman" that can serve as an ideal for all of us, male and female alike, as we strive to grow in discerning wisely:

Affirming that she is strong enough to stand apart liberates a woman. For most women this demanding freedom is only slowly won. Long relied on by other people, a woman gradually comes to count herself reliable. Her intuition, proven trustworthy over time, becomes a credible resource. Now she knows her insights can be trusted. In her own life, experience has ripened into wisdom.

Supported by this strength, a woman approaches decisions differently. Now when complex issues of meaning or value or choice arise, she draws on a new authoritative perspective—the seasoned insight born of her own experience. Other sources of information are not simply ignored, but she weighs their claim more carefully. Confident in her personal convictions, she is not easily dismissed.[30]

In sum, there are no facile methods, no gurus who can tell us ahead of time how to choose life by following God's lead in all the different situations we encounter. Anthony de Mello writes:

To a disciple who was always seeking answers from him the Master said, "You have within yourself the answer to every question you propose—if you only knew how to look for it." And another day he said, "In the land of the spirit you cannot walk by the light of someone else's lamp. You want to borrow mine. I'd rather teach you how to make your own."[31]

Personal Reflections and Spiritual Exercises

A. A Prayer

Lord, I want to decipher your presence
    through the events and objects
    that make up my life
    to express the impact
    that they have on me.
In this I am an interpreter of your creation.
I make use of images, signs, and comparisons,
    and I try to interpret your revelation
    in the daily events that surround me.
All along I am faced, Lord,
    with the mysterious signs of your passing by.
Permit me to see your footprints in my life,
    and to experience the joy of your presence.
Lord, events and objects sometimes pose questions
    and I have no answers.
Grant me some of your infinite capacity
    of seeing and proclaiming
    the truth and beauty
    of the beings you have created.
I want to absorb their message, Lord,
    in order to return them transformed
    into a conscious gift to your love,
    and thus proclaim your praise.
Amen.

                           —Author Unknown

B. Noticing Experience:
The Gestalt Continuum of Awareness

Sit quietly and take some time to be attentive to your present experience, from moment to moment. Just be an observer of your awareness and notice where it goes.

Follow the spontaneous flow of your awareness. Say to yourself, "Right now I'm aware of_____" *(complete the sentence with whatever you are aware of at the moment)*.

Continue to report what you are aware of from moment to moment for about ten minutes, examining the following aspects of your inner being.

What are you aware of in terms of your...

- bodily sensations (tightness in your stomach? tension in your neck? a backache?)
- feelings/emotions (anxious? sad? peaceful?)
- perceptions (what are you seeing? hearing? touching? smelling?)
- mental activities (thoughts? worries? concerns? hopes? fantasies?)

For example,

"Right now, I'm aware of feeling excited about trying this exercise."

"Right now, I'm aware of a slight tension in the small of my back."

"Right now, I'm wondering how comfortable I'll be with this practice of awareness."

"Right now, I'm thinking that this might be a quick way to center myself and focus on the present."

IV.
IMAGES OF GOD
AND DISCERNMENT

Picturing God must precede any speaking about God, for our pictures
accompany all our words and they continue long after we fall silent
before God. Images–the language of the psyche–are the coin of life;
they touch our emotions as well as our thoughts; they reach down into
our bodies as well as towards our ideas. They arrive unbidden,
startling, after our many years of effort to craft them.
　　　　　　　　　　　　　—Ann Belford Ulanov, *Picturing God*

"SHE WOULD HAVE BEEN a different person, if she had had a different God," lamented a woman about her recently deceased
friend who lived a God-fearing, though severely repressed and
unhappy, life. How we perceive God dramatically influences
how we see ourselves and how we think about life. Consciously
or not, our God-images directly affect the way we think, feel,
and act. That is why reflecting on our images of God is so
important when discerning about important life choices. "If
we are ever to reach through our God-images to the God who
breaks all our images," states Jungian analyst Ann Ulanov,
"then we must begin with our own pictures of God—noticing
them, embracing them, housing them."[1]

　　Commenting on the parable of the talents in the Gospel
of Matthew (25:14–29), John Westerhoff illustrates the

direct relationship between our image of God and our behavior. As the story goes, a property owner about to go abroad summons his hired help and entrusts them with his assets. To one he gives five talents; to another, two; and to a third he gives one. In his absence the first two workers double the talents that they were responsible for managing. When the owner returns, he is delighted in their twofold gain and praises them for being trustworthy. When the third worker returns only what he had received, the owner harshly criticizes his performance. In his own defense the third worker argues that the owner's reputation for being a harsh and demanding taskmaster made him so fearful that he buried the one talent in the ground for safekeeping. Calling him wicked and lazy, the owner complains that at the very least the worker could have deposited the talent in a bank and accrued some interest. "This parable about faith or perception," Westerhoff concludes, "confronts us with the subversive contention that the only God we are able to experience is the God we image."[2] Departing from the more common understanding of this parable as a teaching regarding stewardship or the responsible use of our God-given talents and resources, Westerhoff's analysis underscores how our perception of God directly influences our behavior:

> Let us suppose that the first two characters are what we call in literature "throwaway characters." That is, they are included in the story to heighten our awareness of and draw a contrast with a third person. Now in this particular parable, each person has a perception of God and God's nature and character. Recall that when their master (God) returns, the first two report what they have done, expecting that the master will be pleased. They have acted on their perceptions of God, and God praises them. However, the third explains, "I

perceived that you were a harsh, demanding, critical parent, which I hope helps you understand why I did what I did." And God responds, "You perceive that I am a harsh, demanding, critical parent? Well, in that case, I will take from you what I entrusted to you and give it to the others who perceived me as generous, forgiving, and loving and then cast you into a place where there is gnashing of teeth."

This creative interpretation finds support in perceptual psychology's central tenet that behavior is a function of perception. "Modern perceptual psychology," states psychologist Arthur Combs, "tells us that a person's behavior is the direct result of his perceptions, how things seem to him at the moment of his behaving."[3] Our images of God are critical to our religious experience because we meet God as the one we image God to be. Paying attention to our perceptions of God, therefore, is critically important for sound discernment. As Christians, our discernment process cannot help but be flawed if our images of God and perception of the divine are distorted and incompatible with the revelation of Jesus.

GOD AS ILLIMITABLE MYSTERY

To assert that God is illimitable Mystery is to acknowledge that we cannot understand God because God utterly transcends everything we know in the created world. As contemporary theologian Elizabeth Johnson states succinctly:

> In essence, God's unlikeness to the corporal and spiritual finite world is total; hence we simply cannot understand God. No human concept, word, or image, all of which originate in experience of created reality, can circumscribe the divine reality, nor can any human

construct express with any measure of adequacy the mystery of God, who is ineffable.[4]

A Sufi story called "The Blind Ones and the Matter of the Elephant" nicely conveys how the mystery of God goes beyond human comprehension. Once there was a city whose inhabitants were all blind. A hostile king and his army set siege to the city and encamped in the desert. To intimidate his enemies, the king used a mighty elephant in attack. The sightless citizens of the city, anxious for information about this elephant that they would have to defend against, sent scouts to investigate. The blind scouts, knowing nothing of the form or shape of the elephant, groped sightlessly, trying to gather information by touching some part of it. Each of the scouts knew something, because each had felt a part.

When they returned to the city, eager groups peppered the scouts with questions about the elephant's nature and listened eagerly to each scout's report. The scout whose hand had contacted the elephant's ear proclaimed that the elephant was a large, rough thing, wide and broad, like a rug. Disagreeing, the one who had touched the trunk proclaimed that he had the real facts. According to him, the elephant's shape was more like a straight and hollow pipe, threatening and destructive. Yet another scout, who had felt the elephant's feet and legs, exclaimed that the elephant was mighty and firm like a pillar. Each of the blind scouts had felt one of many parts. Each erred by mistakenly identifying the particular part that he had experienced with the entirety of the elephant. The Sufi teaching that is drawn from this tale of the blind people and the elephant is that "knowledge is not the companion of the blind. All imagined something, something incorrect. The created is not informed about divinity. There is no Way in this science by means of the ordinary intellect."[5]

While affirming that God is always more than the human mind can ever conceive or imagine, Christian tradition has simultaneously acknowledged that we have some access to understanding God based on God's loving self-disclosure to us in creation and scripture. God's self-manifestation is contained in the book of creation, especially in human beings who are made in the image and likeness of God. To believe that the Divine has become incarnate is to believe that we live in a world that is dredged in divinity, soaked in God. It is to believe with Elizabeth Barrett Browning that "every common bush is afire with God." Or, as Jesuit poet Gerard Manley Hopkins reminds us, "The world is charged with the grandeur of God. It will flash forth like shining from shook foil." The fingerprints of the divine Artist cling indelibly to the works of God's hands and can serve as clues to recognizing the divine presence.

Christian faith also affirms that divine self-disclosure has occurred in a history that reaches its high point in the person of Jesus Christ. In the life and preaching of Jesus, aspects of the mystery of God are revealed to us. "Jesus is, for us Christians, the decisive revelation of what a life full of God looks like," states contemporary biblical scholar Marcus Borg. Jesus is, in Borg's pithy phrase, "the decisive disclosure and epiphany of what can be seen of God embodied in a human life."[6] In short, God can be contacted through images and symbols because the Creator is manifested in created things. Above all, God's face has been shown in Jesus, the living icon of God. As the late Jesuit theologian Karl Rahner nicely put it, "The center of my theology? Good Lord, that can't be anything else but God as mystery and Jesus Christ, the crucified and risen one, as the historical event in which this God turns irreversibly toward us in self-communication."[7]

When we acknowledge the ineffable mystery of God, we become free to examine our God-images carefully and to ask whether they serve us well in our attempt to live vibrant lives of Christian love. If flawed images of God constrict our freedom and dampen our embrace of life, "new images which ground hope and support transcendence can emerge from the imagination once...[we] surrender to the mystery of God. Images at one point are given up only to be reclaimed with the realization of their inadequacy and yet their indispensability for cherishing the experience of the sacred."[8]

THE GOD OF OUR DISCERNMENT

Being clear about the underlying image of God that influences our discernment requires critical reflection. "Our God-images are as idiosyncratically personal as is our handwriting, our breathing, or our walking," states Ann Ulanov. Our images reflect the influence of our elders, parents, teachers, our cultural and religious traditions, "and our sense that through them a mysterious force is present, transcending all of them as it makes itself known to us. We may come to call this presence God." As "an imaginative cloaking of the invisible through the visible," our God-images can play an important role in facilitating our experience of God, but the "catch remains whether we see through the visible to the invisible or succumb to what religions call idolatry by arresting our gaze at the images we authored. Then we worship gods of our own making and soon exhaust them."[9]

As image-making creatures, we use the stuff of everyday life to create pictures of the ineffable Mystery of God: "Unlike God, we do not create out of nothing but out of what is given us and what we find lying around. Bits of mother and father appear in our God-images. Bits of treasured nature, such as light and darkness, wind and storm, dew and fire, turn up accompanying Yahweh or Christ."[10] What is important is that we see through our God-images to the God beyond them. "Each man creates his own image of God," according to psychoanalyst William Meissner, "even though that personalized and individualized image is in contact with and in dialogue with a shared set of communal beliefs, which delineate the concept of God to which the group of believers pledges adherence."[11] Sometimes our core image of God contains internal contradictions, as with a college student who wrote the following reflection:

> My parents and teachers have painted God out to me as being a happy, loving, welcoming force. I feel like at times I can feel God's forgiveness and love when I do something wrong. My personal images of God are of a larger-than-life faceless figure that has the power to do anything he wants but chooses only to love and cherish us all. My insight is that God loves us all and only wants the best for us, *but he is the wrong guy to make mad!*

With an image such as this, one would be naturally hesitant and cautious in making choices, not wanting in any way to make God mad!

Going beyond the observable influence of parents and teachers who communicate their understanding of God to us, the process by which we form our images of God is a complex one that originates in the infant's unconscious mind, according to some psychoanalysts. Object relations theorists, for example, trace the formation of one's God-image, as well as one's image of self and others, to the infant's earliest interaction with its primary caregiver, generally its mother. *Object* refers primarily to the significant people in our lives, who, in our interactions with them, shape who we are and how we view reality, ourselves, and others. If as infants we experienced our mother's countenance mirroring us as lovable and delightful, we acquire a subjective sense of our worthiness and construct an internal pattern of interacting with others as good, nurturing, and affirming. If, on the other hand, our subjective experience of our mother was one of indifference, rejection, or disregard, the result is a negative image of self and a sense of reality as unresponsive, uncaring, and untrustworthy. In this way, according to object relations theory, our images of God and pattern of relating to others are formed in earliest childhood.[12] Thus, to be more aware of negative or problematic God-images that impede the lifelong process of mature growth, we need to consider how our developmental history has shaped those unhelpful images. Writing on the impact of developmental history on adult religious experience, Stephen Parker states:

> Recognition of the role of developmental influences in experiencing the Holy Spirit requires that one conceive of discernment as a process that includes identification of developmental influences. Furthermore, any view of discernment as a simple process of sorting human from divine influence (as though these factors are unrelated and easily recognized and separated) must be abandoned. A dichotomous thinking that sees claims attributed to divine guidance as either the Holy Spirit or simply products of developmental history fails to grasp the complexity of such processes.[13]

OUR PROFESSED AND OPERATIVE IMAGES

Sometimes the image we verbally profess is not really the image that holds sway. It is not uncommon for our professed image (what we consciously believe and say is our image of God) to deviate greatly from our operative image (the actual image that influences our thoughts, feelings, and attitudes). Gerard W. Hughes, an experienced Jesuit retreat director, provides a clear example of this in recounting how prayer helped someone to uncover a distorted image of God hidden in the cave of his unconscious. Fred, considered a model Christian by all who knew him, was a young, dedicated professional who also found time to contribute actively to civic and church organizations. He kept up an intelligent interest in theology and lived a simple lifestyle, rarely going out to eat and spending little on entertainment. He and his wife spent most of their vacations going to conferences and workshops. On one vacation he decided to make an individually directed retreat. His Jesuit director encouraged him to pray by using his imagination to enter various gospel scenes as if they were occurring in the present and he were an actual participant. Called Ignatian contemplation, this form of prayer invites us to use our senses and imagination to immerse ourselves into a gospel mystery so totally that we receive an intimate, felt knowledge of Jesus that goes far beyond something merely abstract and impersonal.

Contemplating the wedding feast of Cana one day, Fred saw tables heaped with food, set out beneath a sunny blue sky. The mood was festive, the guests were dancing, and the music was joyful. When asked by the retreat director, "Did you see Jesus?" he answered, "Yes." He then went on to describe Christ sitting upright on a hard-backed throne, garbed in a white robe, a staff in his hand, a crown of thorns on his head, with a disapproving look on his face. The appearance of this stern-looking Jesus at a fun-filled celebration jarred Fred into pondering what was being revealed to him in this prayer about his perception of Jesus.

Ignatian contemplation can be a powerful way of hearing the word of God being addressed to us in the present. Like dream-work, it can put us in contact with parts of ourselves that we have unconsciously repressed. In Ignatian contemplation we can be surprised by the sudden emergence of repressed aspects of our selves demanding attention. Such was the experience of Fred in this prayer experience that revealed how his professed image of God clashed dramatically with his operative image. The image of Christ that surfaced spontaneously in his prayer revealed much that had been previously hidden from him about his basic image of God and of Christ. Prior to this prayer experience he probably would have professed that his God was a God of love, joy, and compassion. But deep down in his unconscious, another image of God was influencing his life and choices. Reflecting on his image of a disapproving Christ, he began to understand why he had chosen to structure his life in such a dutiful yet drab way. The Christ of his contemplation was one who frowned on fun and demanded an unceasing application to good works—a dominating Christ who did not allow the simple pleasures of life, like having a good time at a friend's wedding. He slowly admitted something that he had long suspected but kept hidden in his heart: his numerous commitments to good works gave him no joy but were driven by guilt and the fear of a demanding God. This discovery was initially very painful for Fred, but it was the graceful beginning of liberation from a tyrannical image of God.[14]

RECOGNIZING DISTORTED IMAGES OF GOD

Fred's experience is not uncommon. Many of us are unconsciously influenced in our choices by distorted images of God. Sometimes these distorted images are the result of negative transference, the psychological process by which we unconsciously bring feelings from a past relationship into another relationship. Transference, for example, explains how people who were raised by overly controlling parents often end up with a distrustful and rebellious attitude toward authority figures and God, who are perceived by them as domineering and oppressive, much like their own parents.

A former spiritual directee's story vividly illustrates how a distorted image of God can arise from childhood woundedness:

> The only way I can make sense of the present is by looking back at the past. I grew up in a small town in El Salvador where the church was the cornerstone of the community. My grandfather was the church secretary, and he made my religious education one of his priorities. Everything was going as planned until the day he cut his forehead working in the fields. According to local legend, I asked what had happened and he said that the priest had hit him with a stick. I was young at the time and my grandfather was not known to joke while he was sober, so I took his words seriously. The next Sunday I did not walk to church with him. Instead, I waited until everyone had left, and then I fetched his walking stick from the closet. I entered the church through the side entrance with the stick in my hand. I walked down the aisle in full view of everyone in the church. When I was a few feet away from the priest, I raised the stick with my right arm and readied myself to bring down my wrath onto a bewildered man. Suddenly my uncle grabbed me from behind and whisked me outside. The priest was furious. It was as if I had tried to strike God himself, and he banned me from church for two weeks.
>
> This was the most defining experience of my life, and it had a significant impact on my attitude toward

religion and my assumptions about God. However, through the years I have gained a great deal of knowledge that has helped me understand the nature of my spirituality and its development after its mischievous beginnings.

My childhood blunder certainly hindered my religious growth for many years. After being scolded by the priest and banned from attending Mass, I started to fear the church and the clergy. I continued my trips to Mass on Sundays out of love for my grandfather, but I felt that I was an unwelcome visitor in the house of God. Also, I no longer willingly accepted religious instruction, and I started to become more critical of priests and the Bible.

Because I had stopped trying to understand the messages of the Bible, I learned very little about the teachings of Christ and the traditions of the church. Instead, I began to conjure up my own ideas about life, death, and the nature of God. For a period of time I strongly believed that God had created human beings in his image and then started to punish them when he realized they were far from perfect. Today, I know that I was just taking feelings and emotions from my experiences with the priest and transferring them to my relationship with God. As a result, I stood before a God created out of the shame that I felt and the fear that I tried to hide. This was not the forgiving creator of the gospel but an image of a priest whom I hated.

Distorted images can also arise from the psychological process called projection. Projection is a defense mechanism by which people unconsciously disown or deny unwanted feelings, attitudes, and traits by assigning them to others. Projection can impede true discernment by destroying the freedom we are all meant to enjoy as children of God. Just as we project unwanted attitudes and emotions onto others, we also project them onto our image of God. Speaking of this kind of projected image of God, J. B. Phillips states: "A harsh and puritanical society will project its dominant qualities and probably postulate a hard and puritanical god. A lax and easy-going society will probably produce a god with about as much moral authority as Father Christmas."[15] More recently, Donald McCullough has illustrated how our projection-prone minds have created "manageable deities" or gods we can control.[16] These diminutive gods of our own making reflect the utter inability of the human mind to comprehend the illimitable mystery of God. The psychological phenomenon of projection, therefore, exposes us to the danger of imaging a god with attitudes, feelings, and traits like our own—and with the same blind spots.

Such images are naturally distorted and consequently easily destroy the possibility of mature Christian obedience. For example, when our dominant image of God is that of a merciless tyrant, our corresponding response of obedience can only be servile. When our dominant image is that of resident policeman, then our response can only be fearful. When it is that of a judge, then our obedience can only be guilt-ridden. And when it is that of a demanding parent, obedience tends to be infantile or childish. The connection between our father or parent-image of early childhood and our later conception of God is obvious, especially in those of us who exhibit an abnormal fear of authority or an apprehensive attitude toward God. Destroying the possibility of a free and loving surrender to God's influence, this fear can often be traced to the tyranny of a dominating parent. When it is not recognized as the result of a false image of God and is permitted to dominate our religious consciousness, it undermines Christian obedience, which has nothing to do with being fearful, servile, childish, and guilt-ridden.

A classical example of a distorted image of God based on projection can be seen in the myth of Prometheus, the legendary initiator of human culture. For stealing fire from the gods and sharing it with human beings, Prometheus, son of a Titan (the giant elder gods of Greek mythology), was punished by the gods, who feared the development of human beings as an encroachment. Setting God and human beings in opposition, the Promethean myth reveals how false gods are easily fabricated out of human projection. "He knew no god that was not an enemy," notes Thomas Merton, "because the gods he knew were only a little stronger than himself, and needed the fire as badly as he needed it."[17] In order to exist, these Promethean gods had to dominate him. Blinded by his own presuppositions, Prometheus failed to see that fire was his for the asking, a gift of the true God, who created it expressly for human beings.

GOD AS "THE MORE THAT IS RIGHT HERE"

Dietrich Bonhoeffer's paradoxical description of God as "the beyond in our midst" pithily affirms the Christian belief in the transcendence and immanence of God, as does Marcus Borg's naming of God as "the More that is right here."[18] Both descriptions serve to correct a popular misunderstanding that equates divine transcendence with spatial distance. When we say that God is a transcendent being, we mean that God is wholly other, distinct from all created beings. Transcendence in no way implies that God is a distant deity with minimal contact and interest in us. A remote and uninvolved deity reflects the God of deism, who "created the universe and set it in motion but then left it to its own devices, offering no further enlightenment or guidance....[Like] an absentee landlord, this is an 'absentee

God'...remote, aloof, uncaring. Such a God, in practice if not necessarily in theory, is experienced as impersonal."[19] In contrast, the Judeo-Christian faith believes in a theistic God, whose intimate and active presence in creation can be counted on for loving care and guidance. Far from being a distant and disinterested deity, our transcendent God, as revealed in scripture, is the loving Creator of Genesis, the faithful Liberator of Exodus, and the merciful Abba of Jesus. Unfortunately, these biblical images have been eclipsed by aberrant images. The Promethean picture of distant gods antagonistic to humans exemplifies such a misrepresentation. The unequivocal message of Jesus can be reduced to this: the Creator of the universe and the Lord of history is forever and unambiguously for us, on our side. This message constitutes the core of the Christian gospel. To obfuscate this central truth is to garble the good news proclaimed by Jesus.

To say that God is "in our midst" or "right here" is to affirm God's immanence. *Immanence* comes from the Latin *manere,* meaning "to remain within," as distinct from "to go beyond or outside," which is the root meaning of *transcend.* Traditionally predicated of God to express the belief that the divine is to be encountered within the created universe, the notion of divine immanence has been given a variety of interpretations throughout history. In asserting God's immanence, some have slipped into pantheism by holding that God and the universe are identical. Christian theology has always rejected all forms of pantheism as unacceptable because it does away with the absolute qualitative distinction between God and the universe. The challenge throughout the ages has been to affirm God's indwelling presence within the world while maintaining that God is wholly other and irreducible to any aspect of creation. "The religious imagination," states theologian William Lynch, "has fought a long struggle to separate God out from everything else in the world while keeping him altogether present to the world."[20]

The beneficial use of images of immanence for discernment has been well delineated by Edith Genet, a religious educator calling for the need to "respect the creative impulse God has put in us."[21] Images of immanence allow us to visualize God, not as a rival, but as a benevolent presence working in us and with us. As Jesuit Brian O'Leary puts it:

> God is in the process of discernment as the source of our ability to decide in freedom and of our desire to decide with integrity. He is our Creator who continues to sustain us in being and to breathe life into us as we think, reflect, and pray. He is immanent in his creation, in us, and so is acting from within, not from without. God acts from within our human personalities and our lived experience, and especially from within the reality of his graced relationship with us.[22]

Made in God's image, we have been endowed with the ability and opportunity to discover our unique way of collaborating with God in covenant partnership. Having no detailed blueprint for our lives, God leaves open many possibilities for choice. Saint Paul makes this clear when he speaks of the plan of God as a plan of love: "With all wisdom and insight he has made known to us the mystery of his will, according to his good pleasure that he set forth in Christ, as a plan for the fullness of time, to gather up all things in him, things in heaven and things on earth" (Eph 1:8–10). Speaking of God's will as a divine yearning, Ron DelBene conveys well the Pauline sense of God's will as one of love:

> Unfortunately many people view the will of God as rather like a ten-ton elephant hanging overhead, ready to fall on them....Actually the word which we translate into English as *will* comes from both a Hebrew and a

Greek word which means *yearning*. It is that yearning
which lovers have for one another. Not a yearning of
the mind alone or of the heart alone but of the whole
being. A yearning which we feel is only a glimmering
of the depth of the yearning of God for us.[23]

Thus, the will of God is dynamic, personal love urging us
along the path that leads to union with God. As with an ordinary journey, there may be several paths that lead to our destination equally well; or some way may be best; or some way
may lead us away from our destination. So "the prayer to
know God's will," states theologian John Wright, "is a prayer
to have this kind of insight about the choices open to me."[24]
When we pray "your will be done," we are not thinking about
a script of our lives that God has destined from all eternity.
Rather, we are referring to the choices we must make. And
when these lead to union with God, they are compatible with
God's plan to unite all creation. "Thus, it may sometimes
happen that I will actually be doing God's will, following the
guidance of the Holy Spirit, whether I choose this or that."[25]
A conversation between Shug and Celie in *The Color Purple*
makes this point well:

> "Us worry about God a lot. But once us feel loved by
> God, us do the best us can to please him with what us
> like."
>
> "You telling me God love you, and you ain't never
> done nothing for him? I mean, not go to church, sing
> in the choir, feed the preacher and all like that?"
>
> "But if God love me, Celie, I don't have to do all
> that. Unless I want to. There's a lot of other things I
> can do that I speck God likes."[26]

STAYING CONNECTED WITH A COMPANION GOD

The Christian notion of obedience invites us to journey through life staying in communication with the Spirit, the Paraclete. The title Paraclete comes from two Greek words: *para,* meaning "along side of," and *kalein,* meaning "to call." The Latin equivalent of *paraclete* is *advocatus,* from *ad,* meaning "next to," and *vocare,* meaning "to call." Thus, the Spirit is the Holy One whom we call on to stand by our side for support and guidance on our journey. The word *paraclete* also suggests a dynamic way of understanding Christian obedience. The Spirit as Paraclete is a mobile God who walks ahead of us and calls us in all the seasons of our lives to choose life and to embody the love of God for others. Two biblical commandments frame our life of obedience, one from the Book of Deuteronomy and the other from the Synoptic Gospels. First, Deuteronomy makes clear how we are to live: "I call heaven and earth to witness against you today that I have set before you life and death, blessings and curses. Choose life so that you and your descendants may live, loving the LORD your God, obeying him, and holding fast to him; for that means life to you and length of days" (30:19–20). Second, the Synoptic Gospels spell out clearly that fulfilling the commandment of love is the heart of our vocation or calling as Christians. Responding to the lawyer who questioned him about what is required to inherit eternal life, Jesus states, "You must love the Lord your God with all your heart, with all your strength, and with all your mind, and your neighbor as yourself" (Luke 10:25–28; Matt 22:34–40; Mark 12:28–34). By living such a life of love, we shall have life. At each point in our lives, then, we are called to create concrete ways of living and working that maximize our ability to live vibrantly and lovingly. Faithfulness to God's call requires that we stay in conversation with the Paraclete as we discern how best to choose life and to love as Jesus did in the concrete circumstances of our life.

God's expectations for our lives are broad. As Shug puts it, "There's a lot of other things I can do that I speck God likes." Christian discipleship challenges us to pattern our lives on the example of Christ, to whom we are joined through baptism. Like Saint Paul, Christians have been called through grace to preach the good news about Jesus (Gal 1:15–16). However, the distinctive way each of us is called to do this is a very personal matter and may change through the course of time. Changes throughout the life cycle necessitate ongoing discernment regarding the unique work or personal way of life by which each of us is called to glorify God. Because every yes we say entails saying no to other possibilities, we have to choose with care. The Christian ideal is that we submit these choices to God and benefit from the guidance of grace. God's plan for us is not a static, once-and-for-all scenario predetermined from all eternity that exists independently of our inclinations and desires. In the solitude of our hearts and with the wise counsel of others we must choose our particular way at each juncture of our life.

RECONCILING THE EXTERIOR AND THE INTERIOR

Images of immanence highlight the belief that God works through the natural processes (our thinking, feeling, fantasizing, and seeking advice) by which we make our choices. When we earnestly and prayerfully rely on these processes to determine a course for our lives, we can be united to God and see God's will active in us. Some people may find this hard to comprehend if they are used to viewing the will of God as coming from outside themselves or if they see vocation as something decided beforehand by God without any input from the individual involved. In this view God issues a call, and our duty is to respond. This way of imaging vocation as an exterior, one-time call, such as in the cases of Isaiah and Jeremiah, appears in many biblical texts.

However, there are other texts in scripture that suggest an alternative understanding of how God summons people into service. In contrast to an exterior call this view portrays God's call as embedded in one's heart and emanating from one's situation in life. Take, for example, the passage in Exodus about Moses' return to Egypt after a few years in the Arabian peninsula where he got married. In two connecting verses we see an interesting presentation of contrasting descriptions of the same event.[27]

> Moses went back to his father-in-law Jethro and said to him, "Please let me go back to my kindred in Egypt and see whether they are still living." And Jethro said to Moses, "Go in peace." (Exod 4:18)

The very next verse provides quite a different explanation of how it came about that Moses went to Egypt to check on his family:

> The LORD said to Moses in Midian, "Go back to Egypt; for all those who were seeking your life are dead." So Moses took his wife and his sons, put them on a donkey, and went back to the land of Egypt; and Moses carried the staff of God in his hand. (Exod 4:19–20)

The first text leaves the responsibility of the decision to Moses and his understanding of the situation. He assesses things and wants to find out whether his relatives are still alive. The second text, belonging to the Yahwist tradition, attributes directly to God the initiative resulting in Moses' return to Egypt. It bypasses Moses' interior process of evaluating his situation and making a decision.

These Old Testament verses represent alternative ways of understanding how God operates in the world. The latter, based on a transcendent image of God, emphasizes the direct intervention of God in guiding our lives. The former, based on an immanent image of God, sees the hand of God always at work in the people and events that make up our present reality. Corresponding to these two viewpoints, an understanding of vocation can emphasize either the exterior or the interior aspect of the call.

Similarly, New Testament accounts of the call of the apostles illustrate the same thing. Matthew's Gospel, for example, recounts that Jesus, seeing Simon and Andrew, said to them "Follow me" (4:18–19). In contrast, John's Gospel describes the experience of two disciples of John the Baptist being interiorly drawn to follow Jesus. Jesus turned round, saw them following, and asked them what they wanted. They answered, "Rabbi, where are you staying?" "Come and see," replied Jesus. They followed Jesus home and remained with him that day (1:35–39). In Matthew, the initiative is attributed to Jesus. In John, however, the call to follow Jesus is instigated by the prompting of John the Baptist and the disciples' own desire to see for themselves.

Because both approaches have potential pitfalls, sound discernment must balance both views of how God leads us. Overemphasis on vocation as an exterior call can undermine responsible selfhood by fostering the kind of conformity and outer-directedness that easily lead to immaturity. More seriously, an excessive emphasis on an external summons can result in a feeling of being trapped—a feeling that saps all enthusiasm for living. Without free choice, joyful commitment is impossible. Once a Jesuit priest was approached by a man at a busy shopping mall.

"By chance, Father," he asked, "are you a Jesuit?" "Not by chance, sir," the priest responded, "but by choice!" It is this sense of personal freedom that enables people to serve God gladly.

On the other hand, an exclusive reliance on the interior can lead to self-deception and delusion. If we are not open to feedback from others in the faith community, our blind spots can misguide us or lull us into a proud and stubborn sense of certitude that gives the impression that we have a direct line to God. Furthermore, an excessively subjective sense of call may result in weakened commitment and compromise when difficulties arise. Because discipleship always entails a cost, following Jesus with fidelity will necessarily involve some hardship and struggle. During these times our commitment to an interiorly felt sense of vocation can find valuable support in the external ratification of that call by the community.

A Way of Joining the Interior and the Exterior

Reconciling the interior and exterior requires that we take seriously the data emanating from our heart and life situation, as well as the opinion of others who can keep our heart-searching enlightened and free from self-deceit. Honest and integral discernment involves listening to God speaking both within our hearts and in the world around us. A practical way of integrating the ways of interiority and exteriority can be found in the Quaker discernment practice of a clearness committee. Historically, such a committee was used to help couples who were contemplating marriage to look more deeply into themselves and to explore marital issues. However, the Quaker clearness committee has expanded beyond marriage to help members make a variety of important decisions. At the heart of this approach is the belief that "each of us has an inner, divine light that gives us the guidance we need but is often obscured by sundry forms of inner and outer interference."[28] Through caring questioning and careful listening, the five or six trusted people who make up the clearness committee attempt to help the one seeking assistance (the focus person) to discover his or her own God-given lights or inner wisdom. Committee members seek only to help the focus person achieve honesty and clarity regarding his or her own inner truth, not to advise, exhort, persuade, or impose their own answers and solutions. Because the principal goal is to help the focus person clarify his or her inner truth, Parker Palmer insists that "nothing is allowed except authentic, challenging, open, loving *questions* so that committee members do not burden the focus person with their own agenda but help the individual discover his or her own."[29] In this way the committee provides a kind of group spiritual direction. By focusing strictly on their limited though helpful task, members avoid the manipulation that is possible in such group situations. The clearness committee as a method of discernment retains the value of respecting the internal movements of the Spirit within the individual and at the same time offers the community a way of concretely supporting the individual. On one hand, talking things through with a clearness committee guards against uncritical subjectivism on the part of the individual. On the other hand, the prohibition against giving advice and opinions allows the community a way of being supportive without being intrusive.

LIBERATING IMAGES OF THE GOD WHO CALLS

In searching for liberating images of a God who calls us to vocational existence, we are looking for adult images that do not trivialize our freedom and responsibility. If the Christian faith is to speak to us today, it must reject any view of God that would keep adults infantile. This requires the rejection of images of God that have been built on a pattern of deficient relationships experienced as children. For example, a conception of God that is based upon a fear relationship in childhood is not a satisfactory basis for an adult Christianity. We need images that respect both the dignity of God and of human beings.

Integral discernment requires the liberation of God from inhibiting images that arise from projection, transference, and childhood deprivations. These deficient images destroy our ability to live freely as people loved by God. We must abandon the images of a distant and disinterested god, as well as a power-oriented and possessive deity opposed to human desires and development. Instead, we must develop images of God that accentuate the loving generosity of a personal God who not only gifts us with life but is intimately present as a support for the development of that life.

These life-giving images are not new, for they are rooted in the New Testament and reflect the God revealed by Jesus. In the parable of the prodigal son (Luke 15), for example, Jesus portrays God as a forgiving and affirming father. God is like a parent who, without any trace of regret, freely permits us to live our own lives—even though our self-directed journey is often misguided and our return home often tortuous. Unlike the insecure Promethean gods, who viewed human development as a danger to divine status, the God whom Jesus called Abba perennially supports the human effort to establish a life based on the desires of the heart. Sin and misjudgment may retard our progress. What first appeared to be the pearl of great price may turn out to be a fake. But, as the parable points out, God's graciousness provides many chances. We live in a multiple-chance universe, and the effort to root our life choices on authentic, divinely inspired desires must not be abandoned when faltering steps lead initially to failure. Significant learning sometimes only comes through trial and error. Fortunately for us, God, like the father of the prodigal son, allows for trial-and-error learning.

The parable of the prodigal son likens human life to an unrestricted gift that we receive from the hands of a loving God. The Creator gives us time and energy, talents and opportunities to serve through a unique vocation that is revealed to us in our own heart and prayer. But often we do not experience our life as an unrestricted gift and are unsure that God is really behind us. Afraid to trust our hearts, we hesitate and hedge. Yet like the master in the parable of the talents (Matt 25:14–30), God has high hopes that we will fully develop our talents and potentialities. Only when we realize that we are given many chances to live out a loving and God-centered life will we boldly take risks and try out alternatives. Fear of having only a single chance and of losing it through a mistaken choice leads to paralysis and indecision. This fear, as depicted in the parable of the talents, tempts us to bury our assets rather than to invest them with hope for a profitable life. To strive for a vocational existence based on the deep desires of our heart is truly a response to a gracious God's invitation to be co-creators of lives that speak of the marvelous gift and opportunity that human life is.

Personal Reflections and Spiritual Exercises

Window on God: Making Implicit Images Explicit

Purpose

To raise to explicit consciousness the images of God that influence one's life and behaviors.

Procedure

1. Fold a sheet of paper once vertically and once horizontally to form four equal parts. The sheet should resemble an old-fashioned window with four panes.
2. In the first "pane" express with a drawing, symbols, or words God as God has been presented or taught to you by parents, teachers, and friends.
3. In the second "pane" express (once again through a drawing, symbols, or words) the image of God you have formed from your own experiences or personal search. Here you might describe moments when you experienced God in prayer, whether in happy or difficult times.
4. In the third "pane" express the image of God that actually influences your decisions and choices.
5. After finishing the three "panes," study your page and note what the juxtaposition of the three images stirs up in you in terms of insights, questions, and feelings.
6. In the fourth "pane" jot down how your images of God affect your process of discernment.

Process Questions

When you have completed your window, dwell with what you have put down and reflect on these questions:

- What is your *operative,* as opposed to your professed, image of God? In other words, what image(s) actually influences the way you think, feel, and act as a Christian?
- In your operative image is God distant or near?
- Does your operative image help or hinder your spiritual growth, your sense of self and personal maturity, your sense of freedom?

Comments on the Exercise

The value of this exercise is that it can help us see how inconsistent we often are in the way we view God. At times our image of God reflects the maturity of adult faith because it is based on personal religious experience and theological reflection. At other times, our conception of God is still influenced by the outdated notions of God that we acquired uncritically in early childhood and adolescence. Realization of this discrepancy can foster adult obedience by ensuring that the image of the God we obey matches more closely our adult understanding than those images we acquired as children. In the ordinary course of faith development, maturity comes when our image of God is less filled with projected matter from the past and more flexibly formed by the present revelation of the living God, who is "beyond all knowledge" (Eph 3:19).

V.
DESIRES AND DISCERNMENT

*To attend to desires and to discern among them
are parts of the process of becoming more
passionately focused on what is life-giving.*
—Philip Sheldrake, *Befriending Our Desires*

*Trust in the LORD, and do good;
so you will live in the land, and enjoy security.
Take delight in the LORD,
and he will give you the desires of your heart.*
—Psalm 37:3–4

TO LIVE VITAL AND PASSIONATE lives requires that we pay serious attention to our desires when discerning life choices.
Choices that are based merely on external norms and objective values may seem sensible but will feel soulless if they do
not honor our desires. Desires reflect the longings of our
heart and point to an incompleteness yearning for fulfillment. Desires make our life dynamic, keeping us keenly on
the lookout for new possibilities and encouraging us to risk
letting go of the "well-being" of the present for the sake of
the potential "more being" of the future. They energize us
and move us to engage with life in hopes of finding satisfaction. If we leave out desires, we are likely to feel detached,
apathetic, and uninvolved in what we choose. If the glory of
God is, as Saint Iranaeus stated, the human person fully

alive, then desires have a vitally important place in spiritual discernment. Jesuit Anthony de Mello highlights this truth in a story that tells us how we must go about discovering God's call:

> The disciple was a Jew. "What good work shall I do to be acceptable to God?"
> "How should I know?" said the Master. "Your Bible says that Abraham practiced hospitality and God was with him. Elias loved to pray and God was with him. David ruled a kingdom and God was with him too."
> "Is there some way I can find my own allotted work?"
> "Yes. Search for the deepest inclination of your heart and follow it."[1]

Befriending our desires in the process of spiritual growth and discernment, however, does not come naturally for many of us who have been conditioned to be suspicious of desires. A dominant strain of Christian spirituality has traditionally viewed desires as trap doors leading to selfishness and subjective whim. Overcoming desires, especially sensual and sexual ones, is thought to be the true pathway to observing the commandments and living a faithful Christian life.

Contrary to this negative view of desires is the approach of Jesus, who directed people to their desires when they were in search of direction for their lives. John's Gospel (1:30–36) describes the experience of two disciples of John the Baptist being drawn to follow Jesus, who was passing by the Jordan as the Baptist preached his message of repentance. Suddenly Jesus turned around, saw them following, and asked, "What do you want?" Caught off guard by Jesus' question, they replied with what seems like a classic non-sequitur, "Where do you live?" Jesus responded, "Come and see," and they accompanied Jesus home and remained with him for the rest of the day. The Greek word translated here as "remained" is *manein,* the term used in the Johannine literature to connote an intimate encounter or relationship. So, in this intimate encounter with Jesus and in the safety of his home, the two disciples were invited by Jesus to probe the desires that lay deep within their hearts and to share them honestly with him. In light of this biblical text it is easy to understand why Ignatian scholar Philip Sheldrake states that "the key to discernment is not technique but the focused intensity of our desires. It is a matter of attitude and of relationships—the quality of how we relate to our own self, to other people, to created reality, to God."[2]

Appreciating the positive role of desires in spiritual growth, Ignatius instructed people in the *Spiritual Exercises* to begin every period of prayer by communicating their heartfelt desires (no. 48). "Asking for what I desire" *(id quod volo)* is essential to Ignatian prayer. He called this expression of desire a prelude. We can trace the organizing dynamics of the entire *Spiritual Exercises,* an experience aimed at inner transformation, by observing the sequence of these preludes to prayer, which express the desires or the graces sought at each point of the retreat. Ignatian spirituality articulates a spirituality of desire that embraces the goodness of all created reality as well as the goodness of God, who is its Source and Destiny. Contrary to spiritualities that denigrate the things of this life in favor of the blessings to be enjoyed in the life to come, Ignatian spirituality is earth-affirming.[3] Ignatius invites us to perceive all that exists as genuine gifts from God to be enjoyed insofar as they contribute to lives of love now and into eternity. If all created things are good, an attraction to them in desire can be seen as a natural recognition of their goodness. Thus, desire affirms the goodness of creation. The crux of choosing among the goods of creation, for Ignatius, lies in distinguishing between the goods that lead us toward love and the ones that lead us away from love. Briefly stated, Ignatius's spirituality of desire tells us to love God in all things and all things in God.

Ignatius writes that to love God in all things is to have a graced intuition that everything not only comes from God as gift, but that God dwells intimately in all that exists (nos. 234–35). Writing in her journal, a student in a course on Ignatian spirituality expressed with poetic beauty what it means to find God in all things:

> God is the rain that pours down to nourish the earth, and the rainbow arched across the sky after the rain. God is the bud beginning to sprout from the soil and the centuries-old Sequoia tree pointing toward the endless sky. God is the waterfall, overflowing with life and love, pouring it out for me beautifully and powerfully. God is the sparkle in my eye, the story behind my smile, the melody in my laughter, and the spring in my step. God is the outstretched hand, the warm embrace, the pat on the back, the stroking of my hair, the warmth of the sun on my skin. God is the knowing, the not knowing, and the wanting to know. God is passion, freedom, truth, beauty, and love. God is a kind word on a rough day and a letter from a loved one far away. God is the familiarity of the now and the uncertainty of the future. God is home. God is the friend who is always there for me, who challenges me, believes in me, and loves me fully for me. God is the lucky break that I don't quite deserve but am thankful for anyway. God is food on the table, a new day of life, water for a shower, clothes to wear, books to read, and a bed to sleep in. God is learning and teaching, running, playing, singing and dancing. God is friendship and a surprise phone call. God is riding in the car

with the windows down, wind in my hair, singing to
the radio. God is the person I struggle to accept,
struggle to love, and struggle to appreciate. God is the
part of me that I struggle to accept, struggle to love,
and struggle to appreciate. God is the pieces that
seem to fall into place, and those that fall out of place
and make me search for a better way. God is the lesson
in mistakes and the wisdom in trials. God is the letting
go, the deepest desire. God is my talents and gifts, my
hands, my feet, my voice, calling me to action—to
serve, to live out God's dream for me and the world.
God is the dreamer and the dream, the lover, the
beloved, the love.

Indeed, God gives us God's very self in creation. By moving
us to embrace the goodness of all created reality, desires are
true doorways to gratitude and love of God from whom all
blessings flow. Accordingly, Jesuit Anthony de Mello states
that "mysticism is felt gratitude for everything."[4]

On the other hand, to love all things in God, Ignatius
tells us, means that we "love no created thing on the face of
the earth in itself, but in the Creator of them all" (no. 316).
When our hearts are spiritually attuned, we desire God as
the only absolute Good that we cannot live without and
value everything else as relative goods. Material possessions, health, relationships, careers, and occupations are all
good things that can contribute to a life of love, but they
become spiritual dangers when they lure us into thinking
that they can deliver the well-being and security we seek.
According to Ignatius, our soul has been seduced by illusion
whenever we become obsessed with any of these created
goods. Twelve-Step spirituality calls this fascination or
obsession an addiction.

Created things, in their attractiveness, are possible
snares. The story of an African monkey trap illustrates how

evolution has not eradicated all similarities to our simian roots. The trap was basically a large gourd with holes carved out on the sides just large enough for an orange or a monkey's hand to pass through. No elaborate system of nets and concealed pits was needed, because once a monkey put its hand into the gourd and grasped the orange, it could not remove its hand without releasing the orange. Based on a "monkey mind" mentality, which always deemed it necessary to hold on tenaciously to the orange, the trap never failed. Even when the hunter, club in hand, stood threateningly near, the monkey would think that it was stuck, never realizing that all it had to do to escape was drop the orange and run away.

We, too, have "monkey minds" that trick us into thinking that we absolutely have to have certain things to be happy, safe, and secure. Tightfistedly, we cling to these things as if our whole life depends on them—as if they, not God, are our source of happiness and the end point of our human journey. We know that our spiritual journey has been sidetracked when we fall into the trap of mistaking ephemeral and limited goods for the eternal and infinite Good for whom our hearts yearn. Spiritual freedom, according to Ignatian spirituality, entails the ability to act on those desires that are compatible with loving God with our whole being and loving others as we love ourselves, and refraining from those desires that militate against loving in this way.

DEALING WITH INORDINATE ATTACHMENTS

While Ignatius taught that the world's created goods were meant to be appreciated and enjoyed as gifts flowing from the hands of a generous and loving Creator, he, nevertheless, warned that these very same things can hijack our hearts and deter us from our destination. Our instinct for life naturally draws us to whatever seems to enhance our well-being. However, things go awry and work against us when our orientation shifts from enhancing life to needing to control life. Describing this spiritually unhealthy shift, Elaine Prevallet writes: "I don't just want to enjoy the goodness of life. I want to own it, to store it up, to expand it and manipulate it for my own purposes....Attachment is, in the first place, an indispensable capacity in the service of human life. But, unhappy fault, often unbeknownst to us it slips into the service of our selfishness and insecurity, and becomes control."[5] When our attachment to created things moves in this direction, it becomes what Ignatius calls inordinate or disordered. Inordinate attachments cast an addictive spell over us and become roadblocks that may bring a premature end to a journey destined for God as the ultimate fulfillment of human life.

LOVE OF GOD ORDERS ALL OTHER LOVES

The Ignatian approach to getting back on track when we have been derailed in our spiritual journey by blindly pursuing created goods is not to devalue them but to reorder their place in our lives. In other words, Ignatius does not suggest a negative, frontal attack on inordinate attachments but recommends that we pray for the freedom to have or not have them depending solely on what will bring us closer to God. For Ignatius, it is the love of God that will restore proper order to all the other loves in our life. When the love of God becomes once more our highest and only absolute good, the reason we want or retain "anything will be solely the service, honor, and glory of" God (no. 16). In the spirit of this Ignatian wisdom about the liberating power of love,

Pedro Arrupe, SJ, former superior general of the Jesuits, once wrote:

> Nothing is more practical than
> Finding God, that is, than
> Falling in love
> In a quite, absolute, final way.
> What you are in love with,
> What seizes your imagination,
> Will affect everything.
> It will decide
> What will get you out of bed in the morning,
> What you do with your evenings,
> How you spend your weekends,
> What you read, who you know,
> What breaks your heart,
> And what amazes you with
> Joy and gratitude.
> Fall in love, stay in love,
> And it will decide everything.[6]

SORTING OUT OUR DESIRES IN PRAYER

Desires can be bewildering. When we look into our heart, we find a jumbled mixture of desires, dreams, hopes, needs, fears, and longings. Some of our desires are compatible with one another; some are mutually exclusive. We also are aware that desires can affect our lives both positively and negatively. Some desires can enslave us and dissipate our energies; other desires have the capacity to generate power and energize our lives. This is why it is important to pray over our desires. "Prayer is the place where we sort out our desires and where we are ourselves sorted out by the desires we choose to follow."[7] Given the plethora of desires that compete for our approval and commitment, we must choose carefully if we want to live as a unified self, not torn apart by competing and divisive desires.

As we sit with our desires in prayer, we try to refine the acoustics of our hearts and hear more clearly the groanings of our being wrapped up in various desires. Discernment, like panning for gold, is a way of sifting through the complex desires embedded in our hearts. The process involves retrieval, evaluation, and selection. We must first dredge up the raw desires of our hearts and accept everything that we have unearthed. Then we must closely examine all our desires and evaluate what is and what is not reflective of the treasure we seek. In order to know what is treasure and what is dross, we need to distinguish among four affective states: the wishful, the instinctual, the tentative, and the definitive. For example, "I wish I would stop smoking" or "I wish I would win the lottery" are expressions of wishful desires. Instinctual desires are expressed by statements such as "I feel like eating" or "I feel like throwing this chair out the window." "I would like" expresses a tentative desire, something we are considering but have not decided upon. "I want" gives expression to a definitive and clear desire.

Wishful Desires

"I wish," an expression of a wishful desire, pertains to the realm of fairy tales and magic. Such a desire relies on the appearance of a fairy godmother or a genie for its fulfillment. As long as wishes remain only wishes, they provide no bridge between themselves and reality.

Instinctual Desires

"I feel like" reflects those parts of ourselves where impulse, emotion, and appetite hold sway. The value of being connected to our instinctual desires is that they provide us with data that are important for proper self-care and healthy choices. When we are disconnected from our instincts, we are cut off from the very root of our being. C. G. Jung, in his commentary on Ignatius's vision of a serpent with many eyes, underscores the danger of being disconnected from our instincts:

> We should fix our attention on the actual content of this vision. Ignatius had seen a snake covered in shining eyes. This is no isolated case, many of my patients have seen a similar image, it is an essential symbol for the lower part of the nervous system, for the sphere of the instincts. This is the root from which the whole psychic life grows. This is why the serpent is a symbol for healing....When man is ill he is severed from his instincts and part of the art of healing is to bring him back to them, so that he can grow on his own roots. Consciousness and ideas, valuable as they are in themselves, cut us away from the essential roots of our being. Ignatius had surely injured his health with penances and constant prayer, so the healing snake appears as a compensation in his vision, but he was not in a position to recognize this fact.[8]

Twelve-Step programs recognize the importance of being connected to basic human needs and instincts when recovering from addictive behavior. They suggest the use of the acronym HALT as an aid to proper self-care. HALT invites us to ask regularly, Am I Hungry, Angry, Lonely, or Tired? Satisfying these basic needs fosters health and contributes to recovery because whenever we are hungry, angry, lonely, or tired, even our best resolutions and intentions go out the window. Weight loss and anger-management programs also point out the role that basic need fulfillment plays in self-control.

"I feel like" can also be the wellspring of spontaneity and play, adding laughter and fun to life. Nevertheless, "I feel like" typically reflects the fleeting and transitory and does not provide the stable ground for enduring emotional commitments. There is a vast difference between what we may feel like doing and what we want to do. "I feel like" resembles "I wish" more than it does "I want." "I want" contains a commitment that is missing in "I feel like."

Tentative Desires

"I would like" shares much with "I want" but is still tentative and unsure. The subjunctive mood of the grammatical expression itself indicates reservations—ifs and buts. "I would like" tells us that the matter is still under consideration. The final decision is up in the air and can go either way.

Definitive Desires

"I want" expresses a definitive and clear desire. Reflecting on our actual behaviors and choices is a concrete way to discover for ourselves what it is we really want as opposed to what we wish, what we feel like, or what we would like. Real desires disclose themselves not so much in our words as in our actions, specifically in the way we allocate our money, resources, and time. More often than not, what we really want is embedded in what we do and do not do.

Shaping Behavior

The experience of someone who struggled for twenty-five years to give up smoking illustrates these four affective states and shows the power of "I want" to shape behavior. The "I would like" state comes across when he states, "I had known for a long time that it would be a sensible thing to do, and in that sense, I hoped for it." However, his "I feel like" state kept change from happening: "The problem was that on another level I still found that the enjoyment of smoking outweighed my sense of abusing my body and therefore myself." The break-through shift to "I want" came several years later when he said, "I do not *want* to smoke. I positively *desire* to stop. I am going to stop." And somewhat to his amazement, he did stop. Reflecting on his experience, he concludes, "Until giving up smoking moved from being a vague aspiration to touching the deeper level of myself where the power of desire could be unleashed, nothing much happened. When it did touch that level, the focused strength of desire had the capacity to enable me to change my behavior."[9]

The important process of sorting out our desires when discerning is illustrated in a spiritual exercise suggested by Ignatius, called "Three Kinds of Persons" (nos. 149–57). Before making a formal choice or "election" within the context of the *Spiritual Exercises,* Ignatius proposes this meditation in order to assess whether we possess the necessary inner freedom or indifference to be truly open to God's lead, wherever it takes us. (Remember that, for Ignatius, *indifference* means that we are not clinging to something in a way that does not leave us open to following the promptings of God in the process.)

Ignatius describes three groups of people who have acquired a sum of money through dubious means. They are all well-intentioned people who want to be close to God, but they differ in their attitude regarding how to deal with their attachment to the money. Those in the first group acknowledge that they are so attached to the money that it gets in the way of being truly open to God's lead, but they find themselves only "wishing" they were different and unwilling to shake the attachment. Despite their lifelong "wish" to be freed of this inhibiting attachment, they find themselves at their deathbed not having done anything about it.

The second group also honestly admits to being inordinately attached to the money. These people "would like to" free themselves of this obstacle. They find themselves open to doing whatever it takes to grow spiritually but stop short of being willing to give up their attachment to the money. In describing alcoholics who are unwilling to give up drinking altogether, but are open to moderating their drinking, Caroline Knapp provides a contemporary illustration of Ignatius's second group of people:

> The story is classic. The struggle to control intake—cut it back, deploy a hundred different drinking strategies in the effort—is one of the most universal hallmarks of alcoholic behavior. We swear off hard liquor and resolve to stick to beer. We develop new rules: we'll never drink alone; we'll never drink in the morning; we'll never drink on the job; we'll only drink on weekends, or after five o'clock; we'll coat our stomachs with milk or olive oil before we go out drinking to keep ourselves from getting too drunk; we'll have a glass of water with every glass of wine; we'll do anything—anything—to show ourselves that we can, in fact, drink responsibly.[10]

The third group includes those who want to get rid of their attachment and open themselves to retaining or relinquishing the money, depending on what they are inspired by God to do. They simply want to do whatever is best for the love and praise of God, no matter whether it means keeping or letting go of the money. In modern terms this Ignatian meditation can be seen as a kind of psychodrama that can provide us with a clear reading on our inner freedom and desires. By identifying with one of the three groups, we find out where we stand regarding what we "really want," as opposed to what we "wish," "feel like," or "would like" in the choices that we face. This information is important as we proceed in the retreat to make a formal choice.

ROOT DESIRES AND BRANCH DESIRES

Margaret Silf's *Inner Compass*, a contemporary guidebook on Ignatian spirituality, suggests a practical way of going about uncovering our deep root desires and distinguishing them from lesser desires. First, we recall the desires we know we have or have had at different times in our lives. Then we probe these desires in such a way that we are led deeper into the underlying longings that these desires are expressing:

> I remember...when I was thirteen, desperately longing for a dog and a bike. These desires were more than just "Christmas wish list" desires; they had some driving passion in them. What was it? When my parents did indeed buy a puppy and give me a secondhand bike for my fourteenth birthday, at first I was delighted, but ultimately the deep desire I had felt still remained unfilled and was displaced by the next heart dream. So if the puppy and the bike were not the real roots of those desires, what was?
>
> Now, in prayer and with hindsight, I can see that in the puppy I was seeking companionship for a lonely childhood, and in the bike the real desire was for a new degree of freedom and independence.[11]

When the desires of our heart are hidden in the depths of the unconscious, we may misidentify what we yearn for and end up feeding the wrong hunger. Those involved in the

Twelve-Step program called Overeaters Anonymous know from experience that their compulsive eating often stems from an unconscious need to fill up an emotional vacuum rather than a need for bodily nourishment. As Geneen Roth, a contemporary author of self-help books on weight watching, wisely states:

> Wanting is the heart's way of saying "Don't stop here, this isn't it." Wanting goes through a process of refinement, if you allow it. It goes from wanting shelter and warmth and enough to eat to wanting work that is fulfilling to wanting to be thin to wanting to be in love to wanting to be rich to wanting to be famous to wanting to be free. But at every turn we have to stop, have to notice the pain, the dissatisfaction of getting what we want. We have to pay attention. We have to tell the truth.[12]

Sound spiritual discernment requires acknowledging that the root longing of our soul is for God, who alone can satisfy our heart's deepest yearnings. Our choices go awry when we displace this heartache for God onto created things, hoping to find in them the lasting satisfaction that we seek. This displacement leads inevitably to frustration because the essential longing of our being far outstrips the capacity of any created reality to satisfy it. Based on her experience with alcoholic recovery, Caroline Knapp paints a realistic picture of this misguided path to happiness:

> Most alcoholics I know experience...long before they pick up the first drink, that yearning for *something*, something outside the self that will provide relief and solace and well-being. You hear echoes of it all the time in AA meetings, that sense that there's a well of emptiness inside and that the trick in sobriety is to find new ways to fill it, spiritual ways instead of physical ones.

> People talk about their fixation with *things*—a new
> house they're looking to buy, or a job they're desperate
> for, or a relationship—as though these things have gen-
> uinely transformative powers, powers to heal and save
> and change their lives. Searching, searching: the need
> cuts across all backgrounds, all socioeconomic lines,
> all ages and sexes and races.[13]

When feeling empty and needy, we are often tempted to fill
ourselves with consumer goods and objects of attachment
and addiction. This path to fulfillment is culturally rein-
forced. As Knapp notes, "The search for a fix, for a ready
solution to what ails, has become a uniquely American
undertaking, an ingrained part of consumer culture." Alco-
holism, she states, expresses "that particular brand of
searching" and is "an extreme expression of the way so
many of us are taught to confront deep yearnings."[14] Resisting this cultural influence, spiritual disciplines help us to
stem the impulse to find a quick fix and to hold our hungers
until we realize what it is for which we deeply yearn.

DEEP DESIRES AND GOD'S WILL

According to Ignatius, all major life choices must be considered in the context of the overall purpose for which God
created us. In his "First Principle and Foundation" meditation (no. 23), a later addition to the original *Spiritual Exercises,* Ignatius teaches that we were "created to praise,
reverence, and serve God" and to live a life of love with
God and others now and forever. Our earthly journey finds
its ultimate fulfillment only when this end is achieved.
Thus, in the Ignatian tradition, it is the preeminent criterion in making life choices. Whatever contributes to our
achieving this end falls within the realm of God's hope or

yearning for us; whatever fails to lead us to a life of love undermines God's desire for us and our happiness. In assessing people's readiness to start the *Spiritual Exercises*, Ignatius himself spent many hours discussing this general goal of human existence and would allow only those who had internalized its truth to begin the retreat in search of what *specific* life path would best allow them to "praise, reverence, and serve God."

Despite the importance given to the "First Principle and Foundation" by Ignatius, its philosophical and jejune wording, as well as its formulaic and routine use by Jesuit retreat directors through the centuries, turned it into an insipid and dry concept, an uninspiring abstraction—no longer the dynamic life stance that Ignatius sought in someone about to start the *Spiritual Exercises*. Attempting to put juice back into a dehydrated meditation, Jesuit Joseph Tetlow has offered a fresh twist to the "First Principle and Foundation." According to Tetlow: "God projects for each human person a concrete contribution to the Reign, a contribution that will simultaneously build up the Reign and fulfill each person in the self. This concrete contribution God creates as an original purpose in each person....Then in that person God raises desires and valuings out of the original purpose that solicit its free enactment."[15] Tetlow's reformulation rests on the belief in God's ongoing creation of us in the present, which Denise Levertov beautifully captures in her poem "Primary Wonder":

> And then
> once more the quiet mystery
> is present to me, the throng's clamor
> recedes: the mystery
> that there is anything, anything at all,
> let alone cosmos, joy, memory, everything,

> rather than void: and that, O Lord,
> Creator, Hallowed One, You still,
> Hour by hour sustain it.[16]

Based on the belief that God sustains us in life at every moment, Tetlow shifts the question posed by the First Principle and Foundation. The question to ponder now is not so much Why did God create me? but rather Why does God keep me in existence in the ongoing present? In other words, what is God's hope for my contribution to God's project on earth by keeping me alive at this point in my life? To come to a felt knowledge of God's present hope for me is to discover an exciting and concrete way of collaborating with God and of fulfilling God's will. The best way of discovering God's hope for us, according to Tetlow, is to honor our recurrent deep desires. In short, Tetlow argues "that we are being created momently by our God and Lord in all concrete particulars and that we are listening to God's summons into life when we let ourselves hear our most authentic desires, which rise out of God's passionate, creative love in us."[17] In this reformulation Tetlow faithfully reiterates a key Ignatian belief, that our recurrent deep desires (the deeply felt "I wants" of our lives) are regarded as important indications of God's will for us. The urgency of Tetlow's conviction can be seen when he advises those who direct the spiritual exercises to

> explore with a capable exercitant how God's project has a blueprint—the passionate, life-shaping desires that God raises in living persons. Point out how important to thousands and thousands of people are the desires that rise in a Mother Teresa's heart—and wonder whether our own authentic desires are not important, too, and to how many. If each of us enacted the deepest desires that God our Creator and Lord raises

in our spirits, then in that moment the Reign of God
would explode among us.[18]

Our heart's deepest desires are like the pearl of great
price or the field with the hidden treasure spoken of by Jesus
(Matt 13:44–46). Once we identify these, we are challenged
to sell all we have to possess them. In the same spirit the poet
Rainer Maria Rilke says, "What is going on in your inner-
most being is worthy of your whole love."[19] To mold a life
around these deepest aspirations makes a meaningful life
possible and galvanizes our spirituality. To base a life on
social expectations and the wishes of others can lead only to
fragmentation. The challenge of ongoing spiritual discernment is to discover, in the different seasons of our lives, what
is our pearl of great price and then to give our heart and soul
to it. To do this is to create the possibility of becoming a unified soul, a person whose life is all of one piece rather than
patchwork. We must carefully observe what draws our hearts
and then choose that with all our strength.

Sound Christian decision-making dictates not only that
we take our desires seriously, but also that we be willing to
discuss them with a spiritual guide. Such a person can serve
as an objective sounding board and help us avoid the pitfalls of confusion and self-deception that can blur what we
deeply desire. According to Thomas Merton, it is important
to appreciate the role of desires as indicators of God's will
and to be honest about these desires in spiritual direction.[20]
Because a real connection frequently exists between our
spontaneous desires and God's will for us, Merton advises
people seeking help from a spiritual director to be genuine
rather than to present a facade. "We have to be able to lay
bare the secret aspirations which we cherish in our hearts,"
he writes, and in this way make ourselves known for who we
really are. He stresses the importance of discovering our

"holy and spiritual desires" because they "really represent a possibility of *a special, spontaneous and personal gift*" that we alone can make to God. If there is some gift that we alone can give, then most certainly, according to Merton, God asks that gift from us and "a holy, humble, and sincere desire may be one of the signs that God asks it!"[21] Merton's point is central to spiritual discernment: our deep longings are important indications of the will of God for us.

LIBERATING THE HEART

Determining the direction in which our heart is drawing us is often a difficult undertaking. Because many of us are out of touch with our own inner world and experiences, we are unable to identify our deepest desires. Moreover, claims British psychiatrist, R. D. Laing, others have long ago invaded our hearts and have installed *their* "shoulds" for our lives. Our hearts are no longer free but are more like occupied territory. Cultural imperatives, parental "shoulds," and superego dictates often drown out the faint stirrings that suggest what we yearn for.[22] Uncovering the invaluable data of the heart can only occur when the self has been liberated from these foreign "shoulds."

Reclaiming the heart's territory is crucial in the struggle for personal freedom and authentic discernment. The loss of inner data provided by the heart is crippling because it strips us of the ability to direct our lives according to the interior movements of God and leaves us vulnerable to the manipulation of exterior forces. A person without access to the data of the heart is like a sailor without a map or a compass. The winds of external pressures rather than the directives of an intelligent heart will determine his or her course.

Liberating the heart requires dealing with whatever obscures the messages it emits.

A common obstacle to monitoring the spontaneous desires of the heart is what psychologists call introjects. Introjects represent the "shoulds" that other people, consciously or not, impose on our lives. These "shoulds" often interfere with our hearing clearly the "wants" of our heart. Our discernment is sometimes faulty because we ourselves do not know what we really want. An introject-filled heart or a tyrannical image of God can keep us in the dark about our own desires. Often a legalistic notion of the will of God may lead us hypocritically to falsify our true aspirations. Discernment is drastically undermined when we think that God is a harsh lawgiver, uninterested in our thoughts and desires, concerned only with imposing upon us a rigid, predetermined plan.

This attitude is challenged by the fact that we are called to collaborate actively with God in covenant partnership. Saint Paul reminds us "we are God's servants, working together" (1 Cor 3:9). As colleagues, we are called to contribute freely to God's kingdom in the world, to advance God's cause. In this collaboration, which is our basic vocation as Christians, we are not merely passive and mechanical instruments. Our loving, spontaneous contributions to God's work are themselves the precious effects of God's grace. "To frustrate this active participation in the work of God," Merton warns, "is *to frustrate what is most dear to his will*."[23] In a similar vein, E. Edward Kinerk argues, in an essay on the place of desires in the spiritual life, that desires can galvanize our spirituality by providing deep and enduring motivation. If we do not take our desires seriously, "if we are timid about our stronger desires for God and his service, we will have failed to utilize the greatest source of human vitality and passion which God has given us."[24]

The spontaneous desires of our heart are valuable clues to the will of God for us. Yet we are often mistrustful of them because we are suspicious of spontaneity. We are "afraid of spontaneity itself," states Merton, "because we have been so warped by the idea that everything spontaneous is 'merely natural' and that for a work to be supernatural it has to go against the grain, it has to frustrate and disgust us. The truth is, of course, quite different."[25] When we fear spontaneity, we mask our desires, sometimes hiding them even from ourselves. This repression of desires hinders the discernment process because only when our desires are brought out of the cave of the unconscious and exposed to the light of day can they be tested. Only through prayerful discernment can we discover which of our desires are authentic indications of God's will and which of them are not related to the purposes of God and therefore incapable of defining a vocation.

DEALING WITH INTROJECTS

According to Fritz Perls, the founder of Gestalt therapy, "an introject...consists of material—a way of acting, feeling, evaluating—which you have taken into your system of behavior, but which you have not assimilated in such fashion as to make it a genuine part of your organism....Even though you will resist its dislodgement as if it were something precious, it is actually a foreign body."[26]

To check for intrusive introjects, we might ask:

- Are the aspirations of our heart being drowned out by our desire to please someone else?
- Do we bury our inner longings by complying submissively with the wishes of others for our lives?
- Do we turn a deaf ear to God's persistent call, heard in the quiet depths of our hearts, to a committed relation-

ship or work because we fear the disapproval of others?

- Where and how do we betray the self by not listening with reverence to the voice telling us about our inner necessity—that is, our vocation?

Introjects endanger us in two ways.[27] First, people dominated by introjects never get a chance to develop their own personalities, because they are so preoccupied with the "shoulds" imposed on them. The more introjects they have identified with, the less able they are to become aware of their own personal needs. Second, introjects can bring about personality disintegration. If people internalize two incompatible concepts (their own desires and the conflicting expectations of others, for example), they may find themselves torn apart trying to reconcile them. This is not an uncommon experience for many today.

DEALING WITH MISDIRECTED DESIRES

Liberation of the heart not only involves ridding ourselves of inhibiting introjects, but also demands that we confront inner forces that can foil sound discernment. These forces represent the unruly passions and untamed urges that inhibit our freedom of choice and cause us to compromise our deep desires. These internal influences are like weeds that can choke the life out of the good seeds of genuine aspirations that are trying to take root in the soil of our hearts. The garden of every human life contains traces of these destructive weeds, because these disordered desires are part of our weakened human condition. The rich young man of Mark's Gospel is a touching illustration of the impeding nature of disordered desires. Loved by Jesus and invited to a closer sharing of life and work, the young man "was shocked" by Jesus' conditions for discipleship and "went away grieving, for he had many possessions" (Mark 10:22).

Contemporary examples of attachments that hinder a free response to God's invitation to partnership are easily found in daily life; for example, the person who abandons a lifelong dream of being a great scientist or doctor because of a craving for ease or an excessive desire for immediate gratification, or the person who suppresses a deep urge to help the disadvantaged because of a desire for worldly prestige. If left unchecked, these impulses diminish inner freedom and lead to the betrayal of self. Self-liberation, therefore, necessitates exposing these desires as lesser goods that distract us from the pursuit of what brings deeper happiness. Facing squarely our deficient motives and not allowing them to interfere with our heartfelt dreams and aspirations are critical to making life-giving choices.

THE NATURE OF AUTHENTIC DESIRES

As human beings we have a multiplicity of desires that compete for our attention and ask for fulfillment. One of the most important developmental tasks of childhood and a hallmark of growing maturity is the ability to evaluate which desires to act on and which desires to suppress. Making healthy and life-giving choices in all areas of life requires that we be able to distinguish between our many desires and discern which of them define our identity. If desires are to give direction to our most important life choices, we need to be able to discriminate between those that are authentic and those that are fleeting. In discussing this sorting-out process, Kinerk proposes four overlapping presuppositions that can serve as criteria to guide us in what is often a confusing task.[28]

First, while all desires are real experiences, they are not all equally authentic. For example, a devout Christian who has been hurt by another might feel both a desire for revenge and a desire to forgive. But he or she would probably judge the desire to forgive as more authentic because the desire to forgive springs from a more profound level of identity. Such a person's reflection might be along these lines: "I feel more genuinely myself when I picture myself forgiving. And I feel out of sync with the person I want to be when I harbor the desire for revenge." The desire to forgive is more authentic because it more accurately expresses what a devout Christian *really* wants, even though the desire for revenge might be intensely felt. Distinguishing between authentic and superficial desires may involve trial and error, because it is often difficult for us to differentiate our deeper desires from those that are more ephemeral.

Second, our authentic desires are vocational. What we want is integrally connected with who we are. Insisting that "the question 'Who am I?' can never be answered directly," Kinerk maintains that authentic desires serve essentially to enlighten our hearts. We cannot know ourselves unless we know what we really want. Only by asking the question "What do I want?" do we begin to sense the nature of our unique role or calling in life. The more honestly we identify our authentic desires, the more these desires will shape our vocational choice. "What do you want?" is precisely what Jesus asked the first disciples in John's account of their call (John 1:35–39). Jesus aided their vocational discernment precisely by inviting them to pay attention to their desires.

Third, the more authentic our desires, the more they move us to glorify God. All of us experience in some degree a restless yearning for God. Whenever we sincerely respond to this longing, we are also responding to the grace of God, who has planted that desire in every human being. Our most genuine desires spring ultimately from this level of ourselves. They may not always be expressed in explicitly religious terms, but they always move us toward giving ourselves to God and others and away from self-centeredness. "At this level," states Kinerk, "the distinction between 'what I desire' and 'what desires God gives me' begins to blur. The more profoundly we reach into ourselves, the more we experience desires which are uniquely our own but also God-given."[29] Thus, heart-searching is key to discernment because God is often the source of the desires that emanate from our hearts. Because self-deception is possible, we need to test our desires and our interpretation of them with others who can provide some objectivity. Nevertheless, in no case can these desires be trivialized or disregarded without seriously undermining the process of discernment.

Fourth, authentic desires are always in some way public. This is paradoxical but true. While our desires reflect what is most uniquely personal and idiosyncratic in ourselves, at the same time, when seen at their depths, they stem from communal values, not just individual ones. In Kinerk's words, "Superficial desires—such as those linked with consumerism—demonstrate all too graphically our cultural narcissism, but more authentic desires always lead us out of ourselves and into the human community."[30] Thus, such desires as those embodying gospel love—to feed the hungry, to clothe the naked, and to utilize our talents in service of others—become more compelling than private concerns. These desires are more authentic because they reflect our true nature as social beings.

These insights into the nature of authentic desires are very useful when struggling with life choices. Sound discernment requires not only that we be aware of the data of our hearts, but also that we know how to interpret that data with spiritual sensitivity. If we are not spiritually discriminating, we make ourselves vulnerable to being misled. Distinguishing between authentic and passing or ephemeral desires enhances our ability to evaluate critically which of our desires are worth building a life upon and which desires should be acknowledged but not lived out.

WHOLEHEARTED WANTING

When discerning which of our desires should give direction to our life, we must also distinguish between "simply wanting" something and "really wanting" it.[31] When we "simply want" something, contends philosopher Robert Johann, our wanting is halfhearted and conflicted. We do not really want what we choose and may realize that, even as we make the choice, it is at odds with our other interests and desires. Consequently, we are inwardly divided and only halfhearted in our choice. The struggle for freedom is not that we do not have ample choices but that we do not really want what we choose. To be free and unconflicted, contends Johann, our wanting must be wholehearted. When we "really want" something wholeheartedly, we are willing to do whatever it takes to achieve it. What we want has to be grasped not only in itself but in its connections with the rest of reality and what it portends for our life as a whole. Important decisions have lifelong consequences for ourselves and for others, some of which cannot be anticipated.

Requiring thought and reflection, wholehearted desiring demands that we step back from immediate goods and pleasures to see where they lead. This means refusing to endorse our initial reactions until their credentials have been checked and validated. A husband who is committed to being faithful to his wife, for example, may realistically choose not to act out his desire to flirt with a woman colleague or to have a nightcap at her apartment after the office Christmas party. He realizes that his fleeting desire for intimacy with her might well jeopardize his deeper desire for marital fidelity. His desire to flirt is not wholehearted because he does not want the possible consequence of sexual involvement.

We must take our desires seriously, since "they provide the only access we have to the worth of things." Johann cautions, however, that taking our desires seriously is not the same thing as leaving them to themselves and indulging them as they arise. Because they are simply reactions to present objects, desires arise piecemeal. Our wantings can never be more than fragmentary, so long as they are not examined for their conditions and consequences. We cannot want something wholeheartedly when our minds tell us that we will not want to finish what we have started. In short, the aim of thought is neither to suppress spontaneity nor to substitute for wants and feelings. Rather, the function of thought is to liberate our desiring from its fascination for fragments and to make wholehearted wanting possible. Reason and emotion are both critical components of holistic decision-making. Excluding one or the other seriously detracts from the validity of the process.

When done earnestly, the process of discernment reflects our desire to live in harmony with God. Even when we do not get it all right, our very desire to open our lives to the guiding influence of God will inevitably draw us closer to God. Thomas Merton expresses the genuine spirit of Christian discernment beautifully in a prayer:

My Lord God,

I have no idea where I am going.
I do not see the road ahead of me.
I cannot know for certain where it will end.

Nor do I really know myself, and the fact
that I think that I am following your will
does not mean that I am actually doing so.

But I believe that the desire to please you
does in fact please you.

And I hope I have that desire in all that I
am doing.

I hope that I will never do anything apart from
that desire.

And I know that if I do this you will lead me
through the right road though I may know
nothing about it.

Therefore, I will trust you always though I may
seem to be lost and in the shadow of death.

I will not fear, for you are ever with me, and you
will never leave me to face my peril alone.[32]

Personal Reflections and Spiritual Exercises

A. Drawn or Driven in Your Life?[33]

• Reflect on those aspects of your life where you feel you are being drawn by personal desires. Thinking about these aspects, do you feel peaceful? challenged? excited? frightened? In prayer, ask God to show you where these desires have their source. Let God affirm and strengthen those responses and feelings in you that have their origins in God's guiding of your life.

• Now consider any situation in your life where you are feeling driven. Can you identify who or what is doing the driving? In prayer, ask God to free you from any recurring patterns of drivenness in your life.

B. Writing Our Own Obituary:
A Way of Clarifying Deep Desires

The following is a possible format for doing this exercise. If you prefer, you may use your own form.

Name, age_____, died yesterday from_____.
He/she was a member of_____. He/she is
survived by_____. At the time of his/her
death, he/she was working on becom-
ing_____. He/she will be mourned
by_____ because_____. The world will
suffer the loss of his/her contributions in the
areas of_____. He/she always wanted to
_____, but he/she never got to. The body
will be _____. Flowers may be
sent_____. In lieu of flowers_____.

- What core values/desires are important in the orientation of your life?
- What aspects of your being aspire to live in you? What aspects do you want to be sure are lived out while you enjoy the gift of life?
- What unlived desires would you most regret at death?

C. Refining the Acoustics of Our Heart

Sifting through the seething mass of conflicting needs, hopes, dreams, dreads, and longings that reside in our hearts can bring clarity and direction for our lives. A simple way of sorting through our affective states is the following sentence-completion exercise:

> Right now, I wish...
> Right now, I feel like...
> Right now, I would like...
> Right now, I want...

Doing this exercise at different times can attune us to what is stirring in our inner life. This exercise is most helpful when our answers are spontaneously and honestly recorded, resisting any temptation to filter or censor our responses.

By reviewing our responses over a period of time, we can notice whether patterns can be seen and what the accumulated data might indicate for our discernment process, and we can consolidate and crystallize what we have gained by completing the following:

- From doing this exercise, this is what I have *learned* about myself and what I want regarding the present choices that face me...
- From doing this exercise, I have *re-learned*...
- In doing this exercise, I was *surprised by*...

D. Learning from the Parable of the Rich Young Man
(Mark 10:17–22)

Mark relates the story of Jesus' encounter with a young
man searching for a spiritual path to eternal life or true,
unending happiness. Responding to the man's request for
guidance, Jesus looked steadily at him, loved him, and
invited him to be a disciple. Not free to say yes, the man
went away sad.

- Reflect on some choices in your present life that you
  feel might contain a call or invitation from God to live
  with more joy, love, peace, freedom, and meaning.
- Imagine that Jesus is regarding you with love, as he did
  the rich young man in Mark's story.
- Ask yourself which of your choices stir up feelings similar to those of the rich young man when he received
  Jesus' invitation.
- Which of the choices before you, if turned down,
  would make you go away feeling sad?

E. The "Crock of Shoulds":
Resisting the Tyranny of "Shoulds"

Purpose
First, to help you to become more aware of the "shoulds"
you are experiencing in the present; second, to recognize
the source of these inner dictates; and third, to clarify how
you wish to respond to each of them.

Procedure
1. Make a list of the "shoulds" you are experiencing in
   your life. Make your statements brief and simple,
   expressing directly what you feel you ought to be doing
   and feeling without giving any reasons or explana-
   tions. Give life to your pen. Be as spontaneous as possi-

ble, trying not to filter or censor what automatically surfaces in your consciousness. Merely record what occurs at each moment. Continue to list these "shoulds" for ten or fifteen minutes. Write whatever comes to mind, even if it means repeating yourself.

2. Look over the list and put a plus (+) next to the statements about which you feel positive, an "x" next to those about which you feel negative, and a question mark (?) next to those about which you have ambivalent feelings.

3. Try to identify the source of the "shoulds" that stir up negative feelings by asking yourself where this "should" is coming from. Can you associate any of these negative "shoulds" with a face or voice? Are these "shoulds" being imposed from someone in the environment, or do they originate in yourself? Perhaps they originally came from someone in the environment but have since been internalized to such a degree that it would be truer to say that the source is within yourself.

4. Once the source of the negative "shoulds" is identified, ask yourself how you want to respond to each at this time in your life. If the source is someone other than you, it could be someone close by, distant, or even dead (since death ends a life, not a relationship). Knowledge of the source will help you decide how you want to—and can—respond.

Comments on the Exercise

The value of this exercise is that it can clarify, for those driven or paralyzed by the tyrannical voices of inner "shoulds," where the battle for personal freedom is to be fought—with someone in the environment or within oneself. If the source of "shoulds" is actually within oneself and being projected onto others, it would be fruitless and destructive to look for a solution outside oneself.

This exercise also helps a person to recognize "shoulds" that elicit positive feelings. Perhaps, it would be more proper to label these as "wants" rather than "shoulds." Desires must be seriously respected in the discernment that accompanies Christian obedience. Writing about the connection between our spontaneous desires and finding God's will, Thomas Merton states: "We must be prepared to take responsibility for our desires and accept the consequences....Such real, genuine aspirations of the heart are sometimes very important indications of the will of God."[34]

Through this exercise, we can also examine those "shoulds" that stir up mixed feelings within us. By reflecting more concretely on our ambivalent reaction to these "shoulds," we can gradually clarify our feelings and decide how we want to respond to them.

VI.
DREAMS AND DISCERNMENT

Natural and necessary expressions of the life force,
dreams provide access into unconscious areas of life.
They give specific and appropriately timed messages,
which can assist the dreamer with problem solving,
artistic inspiration, psychological development,
and spiritual deepening. They are also important
for healing.
—Edward C. Whitman and Sylvia Brinton Perera,
                    Dreams, a Portal to the Source

IN THE CHRISTIAN TRADITION, the notion of vocation or calling has been viewed in two ways. An earlier view of vocation understands God's call as a single event, a static,
once-in-a-lifetime reality that remains unchanged. According to this paradigm God calls each of us once, usually in
young adulthood, to a particular way of life. Once we have
discerned that call, we know with certainty and finality what
God wills for us for the rest of our life. A second, more
dynamic view of vocation has been influenced by a developmental understanding of human growth, which suggests
that just as our bodies change throughout the course of our
life, so do our psyches. An understanding of vocation as
developmental and evolving stems from the realization that
our sense of who we are—our personal identity, our self-

awareness, our psychological needs and desires—undergoes gradual and sometimes dramatic changes over the course of a lifetime. In the former approach God is seen as having a very specific, predetermined plan for each of us, and following this plan is God's will and our salvation. While remnants of this view still linger today, contemporary spirituality understands God's will in a more expansive and invitational way.

God's call to us is ongoing and is addressed to us in the various stages of our life. God may call us many times in our life, and our salvation is not dependent on figuring out a divine plan and conforming to it as docile children. Rather, God is concerned with guiding us at each stage of our life journey as we actively search out paths to living fully. If God's desire for us is, as Saint Iranaeus believed, that we become "fully alive," it follows that God is not concerned with passive obedience. This understanding of faithful obedience holds that God's will for us can very well correspond to our own deep desires. In this paradigm we praise God by realizing the potential that was divinely placed within us and becoming all that we can be. There are many choices open to us at each juncture in our life, and God simply asks that we be faithful to the truth of our own being. Discernment is a way of listening both to God's hope for us and to our own deepest desires. This is where dreams, which emanate from the depths of our soul, can assist us as we discern God's call.

Dreams are a valuable source of inner guidance, whether we are trying to make an important decision or simply trying to grow in self-knowledge and understanding. Each night while we are sleeping the dreaming self is at work gathering from the unconscious information that is relevant to our daytime concerns. When we consciously engage our dreams, it is like working with a wise counselor whose door is always open to us. This means that we never have to rely solely on our common sense or our intellect in dealing with life issues; we also have the wisdom of the unconscious to comment on, or in some way contribute toward, the issue we are trying to resolve. Dreams also help us find solutions to everyday problems. A friend recently told of a dream that directed her search for a pair of lost eyeglasses. Before falling asleep she was feeling frustrated about losing yet another pair of glasses, and she recalled muttering to herself, "I really hope I don't have to replace them." Then she had a dream in which she saw her glasses lying on a carpet. When she woke up, she decided to take the dream seriously and search the house again, but this time she focused on the carpeted floors. Not finding them in the house, she went to her car, and there, on the carpeted floor of the driver's seat, were her eyeglasses, a place she would not have searched had it not been suggested by her dream. By contributing data from the depths of the unconscious, dreams expand our perspective in decision-making, often offering considerations that we in our waking moments would not have seen.

"Messages" from God

Primitive and modern cultures alike have recognized the importance and usefulness of the psychic phenomenon we call dreams. "Thousands of years ago, dreams were seen as messages from the gods, and in many cultures they are still considered prophetic. In ancient Greece, sick people slept at the temples of Asclepius, the god of medicine, in order to receive dreams that would heal them."[1] In the Judeo-Christian tradition dreams have been aptly referred to as the forgotten language of God. Scripture is replete with references to God using dreams to communicate: Jacob is reassured in a dream that God will keep him safe on his journey (Gen 28:10–22); Joseph is counseled in a dream to honor his marital commitment to Mary (Matt 1:20–22) and later, to flee into Egypt to safeguard the infant Jesus (Matt 2:13–14); and the three magi are told in a dream not to return home by way of Herod (Matt 2:12). These and other scriptural examples invite us to include dream-work in our spiritual practice and illustrate the role that dreams can play in the discernment process. The art of dream interpretation, like the art of prayer, is learned through experience and guidance, so the longer we work with our dreams, the more natural it becomes. But no matter how practiced we become in the art of dream-work, it is always enormously helpful to talk about our dreams with a trusted friend, a therapist, or a spiritual director. Even the most skilled expert knows how difficult it is to be objective about one's own personal material.

As is true with understanding scripture, the understanding of dreams requires a contemplative approach. Spending time with the images in our dreams and carrying them in our hearts as we go about our day keep us close to the deeper self and open to its wisdom. If before going to sleep, we pray for a dream that will reveal God's direction in a particular matter, a revelatory dream may be given to us. Recording the dream and bringing it to prayer remind us to ask God for the grace to see what we need and to do what we need to do. Contemplating our dreams is important, but integrating what we learn by bringing it into our life in some way is what makes dream-work fruitful. Just as faith without action is hollow, so it is with dream-work. In discussing the function of dreams, Jung referred to what he called the "moral" function of dreams, which, he said "amounts to a psychological adjustment, a compensation absolutely necessary for properly balanced action."[2] He believed that in order to find the right response or solution to any problem, it is essential to reflect consciously on "all the aspects and consequences" of the problem. Our conscious discernment, he says, "is continued automatically in the more or less unconscious state of sleep, where, as experience seems to show, all those aspects occur to the dreamer (at least by way of allusion) that during the day were insufficiently appreciated or even totally ignored—in other words, were comparatively unconscious."[3]

DREAMS AND SPIRITUAL GROWTH

Dreams take us below the surface and into our spiritual depths. When we pay attention to our dreams and actively work on them, we profess our belief that our inner life matters because it is the place where our treasure lies. Dreamwork builds a bridge between our ego and our soul, or between our waking self and our deepest self. If this relationship is weak or lacking altogether, then we are in a state that psychologists refer to as unconsciousness, a state that is natural for animals and infants but far from desirable in adults. Our capacity for self-reflection is a measure of our spiritual development and psychological maturity, as well as a good predictor of the quality of our relationships. As Jesuit Gerard Hughes states, "When the inner life is ignored, violence erupts in some form or other, whether in physical or mental illness in the individual, or civil unrest within a nation, or war between nations."[4] To see how this happens in our own daily lives, we need only examine our most recent interpersonal experiences with anger and conflict. We have to admit that, at times, we act out our bad moods, nursed hurts, or repressed angers on anyone who rubs us the wrong way. We justify our bad behavior by blaming

others for our bad feelings. Becoming conscious means recognizing that our moods, hurts, and angers belong to us;
they are part of our inner world and, as such, influence how
we perceive the outer world and determine our actions and
reactions to it.

A client's dream illustrates how our inner life affects our
perceptions and behavior. Having grown up with a critical,
perfectionist mother, the client never felt good enough to
be loved. As a protection from the pain this caused her, she
learned to intellectualize her feelings and emotions; she felt
contempt for those who expressed feelings. That she was
angry and resentful, especially toward women, was notice-
able to everyone but herself. Having little awareness of the
connection between the turmoil in her inner world and her
interpersonal conflicts at work, she dreamed the following:
"I am out in public—a busy street. I'm holding a yapping dog
in my arms, and I'm trying to get someone to take it. No one
seems willing to take it. I keep trying to get rid of it—I can't
stand its yapping."

Noreen:	What associations come to mind when you think of the dream?
Client:	The yapping dog reminds me of Judith (a woman at work), who bugs the hell out of me.
Noreen:	How would you describe Judith?
Client:	She's emotional, outspoken, argumentative, aggressive, and a know-it-all.
Noreen:	Is there a part of you that is like that yapping dog?
Client:	Not really.
Noreen:	Well, let's think about it. Dogs are instinctive animals. How do you feel about the "dog" part of you? Might you want to get rid of your instincts, your emotions, and feelings?

Client: Yes. For a while now I've been bothered by compulsive thoughts in the middle of the night. When that happens, I get out of bed and write them down in a notebook. Then I'm rid of them.

Noreen: Has this happened recently?

Client: Several nights ago. The dream came after an intense argument I had with Judith that stirred up all the negative feelings I thought I had gotten rid of. She makes me so mad. I wish I could get rid of her!

After many months the client realized that the yapping dog in her dream was a personification of the part of her she wanted to be rid of. She began to see her contribution to the conflicts with her co-worker and how her rejection of herself and others mirrored the rejection she had felt from her mother. A new willingness consciously to confront the pain and hurt of her childhood made her more compassionate toward herself and had a positive impact on her relationships with others.

Many of us have pockets of hurt and anger that are yet to be dealt with. Conflicts in interpersonal relationships can be a signal that an unprocessed wound is pressing for attention. If we fail to heed this aspect of inner work, we will project our "yapping dog" onto others and try to "get rid of them," because they are now our enemy. This is how feuds and wars are born.

DREAMS AND GROWTH IN WHOLENESS

A main function of dreams is to provide a balance or correction to our waking views. C. G. Jung recounts a dream that corrected his negative attitude toward a patient. His patient was an uneducated, simple woman with whom he had grown bored and hopeless. After one particularly dull session he had a dream in which he was looking up at this woman, who was seated on a wall high above him. When he awoke with a pain in his neck, he realized that his dream, by putting his patient above him, was telling him that in reality *he* felt superior to her and that this was hindering her progress. During their next session he shared the dream and interpretation with her, and this brought about a significant change in their relationship and revitalized their work. This example from Jung's life aptly illustrates the way in which a dream, by revealing a hidden attitude or behavior, can increase our consciousness. Jungian psychology calls this the *shadow side*, a term that refers to all the aspects of us that are unknown to our waking self. In Jung's case the unknown had to do with his unconscious superiority. Like Jung, we all have blind spots that keep us stuck in a conflict or unable to make an important decision. At such times dreams help us by compensating for our one-sidedness, filling in the holes of our self-awareness and showing us unrecognized potentials or areas of inferiority that hold us back. In this way dreams also serve to strengthen our ego and build our self-confidence and, in so doing, contribute to our wholeness.

The story of a middle-aged minister illustrates how dreams can further our growth in wholeness. Having served the poor and downtrodden successfully for many hard years, he was given a sabbatical for rest and renewal. In the course of his year off he spent some time at a spirituality center learning the art of spiritual direction. Surprisingly, he discovered a deep desire to include spiritual direction as part of his future ministry. He intuited that his attraction to a ministry devoted to nurturing the spiritual growth of others was also an invitation to better integrate his own *anima,* the feminine side of his personality. Although such a ministry was in stark contrast to his prior work as a social activist, he experienced it as a call by God, a religious inspiration that needed to be reverenced and honored.

After his sabbatical he had a number of ministry options, some with the possibility of doing spiritual direction and others that would leave no room for it. Among these choices one had an urgent appeal for him. It involved working in an inner-city parish that was engulfed in crisis and floundering badly. He was deeply conflicted. At times he felt the urge to rescue the parish, even though it would be all consuming and leave no time to do spiritual direction. At other times he vigorously resisted the notion of abandoning his newly felt call to a ministry of spiritual direction.

In the course of his discernment process he had a dream that confronted him with his tendency to toss aside important personal needs whenever a desperate situation activated his messianic instinct. Prior to going to bed, he was in his office distributing the personal effects of a deceased colleague and close friend who was highly esteemed by the parishioners. He freely gave whatever each parishioner requested, thinking to himself: "That's me. Whatever people want from me, they can have." Later that night he dreamed that a woman secretary was handing out the personal effects of his deceased colleague. When she got to a statue of the Blessed Virgin Mary, she exclaimed, "No, you can't have this. I need this."

Like the dream that directed the three magi to avoid King Herod on their return home, the minister's dream also bore wise guidance. It was the psyche's attempt to restore balance to a conscious identity that was out of touch with its own neediness and unable to lay legitimate claim to what was required for his own survival and growth. The dream had a compensatory function in that it evened out his one-sided thinking. When he applied its message to his discernment, he felt he was being cautioned against an impulsive suppression of his desire to do spiritual direction, which would also mean abandoning his *anima*, symbolized in the dream by both the woman secretary and the statue of the Virgin. The dream, like a wise inner counselor, reminded him that there are certain values to which he must cling for the sake of wholeness.

THE LANGUAGE OF DREAMS

Dreams are a spontaneous self-portrayal, in symbolic form, of what is happening in the inner world of the unconscious. We might think of dreams as photographs of our inner life, pictures that show us not as we see ourselves but as we are seen by the unconscious. A Catholic deacon recounted the following dream: "I'm working on a parish project and become aware that Jesus is standing next to me, so close that I feel our arms touching. I don't know how to act with him. Should I treat him like God or like a friend? I feel more as though he's a friend. The problem is that I can't seem to shut up and hear him. I am trying to direct what's going on." After this dream the dreamer was able to begin to see the shallowness of his spiritual life. Although he consciously desired a personal and intimate relationship with Jesus, his need for control and his attitude of superiority prevented this from happening. Eventually he saw that the way he was in the dream also mirrored his relationships with his wife, his children, and his friends.

Dreams are one of the best tools we have for self-knowledge because they cannot be filtered or controlled by our conscious mind. Skirting the ego's need to look good and be seen in a positive light, dreams go right to the heart of us, to the soul, where we are before God, warts and all. They "tell it like it is," presenting us with rejected and disowned parts of ourselves and inviting us to grow beyond our comfort zone for the sake of our wholeness and healing. The language of dreams is the language of symbol and metaphor, which for most people requires a new way of thinking, similar to learning a new language. In our waking life we use the language of consciousness; we think in words, we have ideas, we form concepts, and we are logical and rational. The unconscious, however, uses images, symbols, metaphors, and parables, not unlike the method that Jesus often chose to convey his message. This means that the logical mind and rational analysis that may work in other areas of our life will not work in dream interpretation. Since dreams circumvent the intellect's rules regarding order and fixed meanings and present us with the most illogical problems and incredible happenings, there is nothing that is impossible or improbable in a dream.

Dream-work as a Spiritual Practice

In order to benefit from the wisdom of the psyche as it comes to us in dreams, it is necessary that we are both intentional and open in our desire to know God's will. Intentionality in this context refers to having the conscious desire to be receptive to the messages that come from the unconscious in dreams. One practical way of doing this is to pray for God's guidance each evening before going to sleep. Even though we all dream several times each night, it takes a deliberate act of the will to honor those dreams by recording them and interpreting them. Human nature being what it is, we easily grow lazy and resistant to the discipline of writing down dreams immediately when we awaken. Or we record them but fail to devote the time necessary to receive them fully. As with any spiritual practice, dream-work requires discipline and commitment.

A second attitude that is basic in the process of discernment is an openness that resembles Ignatian indifference. This simply means that we strive to free ourselves of biases that get in the way of hearing God's desire for us. As we journey on the spiritual path we discover that our ego's desires and preferences are not always consistent with the deepest desires of our soul. We come to know ourselves as we are, with our mixture of virtues and vices, strengths and weaknesses, self-negating and self-affirming tendencies. Discovering the shadow, that side of us that houses all those parts of us that conflict with our ego ideal, is a humbling experience that teaches us that we are not always what we think we are. We strive to follow God's will, but at the same time we are easily sidetracked and misled into believing that our ego's desires are where our treasure lies. Or, as Saint Paul put it, our unspiritual self is at odds with our spiritual self. Indifference, sometimes referred to as holy indifference, does not mean that we do not care about the outcome of our discernment or that we have no will at all, but that we are willing to put aside the pleasure-seeking demands of our ego in order to discover where true fulfillment lies.

IMAGERY AND INTERPRETATION

Every image in the dream is a representation of some aspect of the dreamer, whether that image is of a known or unknown person, an animal, an object, an aspect of Mother Nature, a vehicle, or a mythological creature. "Dreams, then, convey to us in figurative language—that is, in sensuous, concrete imagery—thoughts, judgments, views, directives, tendencies, which were unconscious either because of repression or through mere lack of realization."[5] We do not need to know a great deal about dream-interpretation theories in order to work with our dreams. Since the aim of dreams is to communicate an important message to the waking self, we can be confident that, armed with a basic understanding of dream-work and using the guiding questions provided at the end of this chapter, our efforts to understand our dreams will bear fruit. Each of us has our own symbols, born out of our own personal history of relationships and experiences, that the unconscious uses to communicate with us. We may not understand all that a dream is saying at first, but when we keep a journal of our dreams, we can look back at them at some later time and see more than we could at the actual time of dreaming.

The full meaning of a dream that initiated Wilkie's midlife vocational discernment only gradually revealed itself as he wrestled with it over several years. The dream occurred in the spring of 1990, during his first year back at Loyola Marymount University after a six-year absence during which time he had served as the director of novices for the California Jesuits. After the initial excitement of re-entry had receded into the routine of academic life, he began to notice the recurrence of a low-grade depression during morning prayer. In his journal he wrote, "I've always been a happy, upbeat person. I'm confused about these feelings of depression. Last night, I had a dream. In the dream, I saw myself in bed in a hospital room with a woman nurse takng care of me. As she worked with me, one of my fingers suddenly fell off." And a few days later, he wrote, "Working with the image of the fallen finger, I realized that the depression was part of grieving the physical diminishment that comes with middle age. I was beginning to experience this aspect of aging. As I often joked with friends, 'my hair is either graying or going.'"

While this realization was helpful, it seemed incomplete. A few weeks later his journal recorded a new insight. "I wasn't satisfied that I had caught the fuller meaning of it [the depression]. Then it dawned on me that the finger is a phallic symbol. As I thought about it, I came to understand the core of my depression and to admit my growing sense of isolation and loneliness in ministry and community. The dream helped me to articulate something that I had been vaguely feeling, but had not acknowledged: a sense that my affective and sexual energies were draining away. What at first was a persistent and puzzling mood of depression eventually became a source of revelation as it led me to explore more deeply what it was that needed my attention and care." As happens with moods when we take them seriously, Wilkie's depression disappeared as he patiently worked with the symbolic content of his dream. As the meaning of the depressed mood became conscious, the energy that had been held down (because that is what is happening in depression) became available to him and he could begin to explore how to integrate this energy into his life.

Because dream images are symbolic and open to multiple levels of meaning, their interpretation cannot be arrived at by a rational, step-by-step methodology. More like parables than scientific or mathematical problems, dreams can have many, sometimes paradoxical meanings. "In the best sense a dream interpretation *suggests* something; it occurs after patiently circumambulating the images; it hits us suddenly and is simply 'there.'"[6] An effective interpretation always reaches us on a feeling level. The idea here is not that we should wait passively for some meaning to present itself, but that we should suspend our usual goal-oriented approach and adopt a more contemplative or meditative one, "patiently keeping company with the dreams and one's hunches about them until one's consciousness changes imperceptibly...and new insights come to light, something new is grasped, the old is elucidated, and what is happening now becomes more understandable."[7]

There is a category of dreams that stand out as "big dreams"; they have such a profound impact on us that we are never the same afterward. These dreams change our self-perception as well as our perspective on life. Five years after Wilkie's dream that initiated a long process of discerning whether to leave the Jesuits and active ministry as a priest, he had a big dream that broke through an impasse in his discernment. Having sorted out and resolved—through prayer, spiritual direction, and therapy—the many personal issues intertwined in such a major life change, he felt strongly drawn toward the choice to leave religious life; however, as he lived with this possibility, questions lingered. "How can I make such a decision and still be faithful to God?" he wrote. "Having taken final vows as a Jesuit, how could it be right to leave, with the desire to live a married life?" This type of inner conflict between head and heart is not unusual when we are in the process of making an important life choice. Nor is it unusual to experience a state of suspension or "stuckness" when we are humbled by our inability to resolve such an impasse. This is where Wilkie stood, unable peacefully to move ahead but also unable to reconcile himself to staying where he was, when he had the following dream: "I was watching a young man saying goodbye to his mother and father, who were weeping and trying to convince him not to leave them. But the young man seemed coolly impervious to their sad pleas and remained firmly determined to go. Witnessing this, I found myself angry with the young man for his unfeeling, insensitive attitude toward his parents' pain. Then, in a flash of insight, I recognized that the young man was I at nineteen, saying goodbye to my parents in Honolulu to join the Jesuits in California. Then a second scenario quickly followed. I saw myself (then at the age of fifty-one) running down the long flight of stairs of my childhood home, sobbing with grief, and heading in the direction of Noreen."

REFLECTIONS AND INTERPRETATION

Reflecting on this dream and its importance in his discernment, Wilkie wrote, "This dream provided a perspective that I had not considered. By weaving the two scenarios into one dream, the dream helped me to see a connection between the past and the present. I began to understand that the decision I had made as a young man to enter religious life and the decision I was struggling to make in midlife were rooted in the same desire to be faithful to a call of God that seemed similarly shrouded in mystery. The dream accurately reflected my agnostic Chinese father's confusion and angry objection to my going off to live an 'unworldly' and celibate life. Somehow, I had the ego strength at nineteen to be undeterred by my father's objections and his threat to sue the Society of Jesus if I were admitted. Just as the dream captured my determination to enter religious life, even if it meant defying a father whom I loved dearly, it also reflected my sadness at leaving the Jesuit order, which had been my home for over thirty years. The dream helped me realize that the calls at age nineteen and at age fifty-one were of one piece: to follow God trustingly into an unknown and scary future that would unfold with God's support. Strengthened by this dream I eventually applied for and received a dispensation from my vows, as well as permission to marry within the Catholic Church. Since then, I have grown in my belief that our commitment to live faithful lives fails 'not when earlier versions undergo change but when we can no longer imagine that God is about something in our life.'"[8] It often happens that when we have exhausted all our conscious efforts to find an answer that will resolve a problem or end an impasse, a dream comes from the deeper self that shows us the way.

COMMON MISCONCEPTIONS IN DREAM INTERPRETATION

Dreams are a popular topic of conversation. It is not unusual to hear people talk about their dreams at social gatherings or to find articles on dreams in news magazines and popular journals. Some articles are scientific, dealing with the function of dreams and the brain activity involved. Others offer suggestions on how to interpret dream images or how to program the mind to dream about particular issues. Several years ago the *Los Angeles Times* ran a weekly column called, "What Do My Dreams Mean?" People sent in their dreams, and two were chosen each week to appear in print along with an interpretation. The column proved to be a helpful, if unintended, teaching tool because it provided examples of dreams that are typical to all dreamers and also illustrated the fact that most dreams contain a large number of symbols, some of which are unique to the dreamer, while others are universal (for example, fire, death, running to catch a train, being chased, packing for a trip, flying). In addition, it highlighted several misconceptions about dream-work.

DISREGARDING THE DREAMER'S INPUT

From a Jungian point of view, the most jarring aspect of the newspaper series was that the dreams were interpreted without the dreamer's associations and feelings, a *sine qua non* of Jungian dream interpretation. "If we want to interpret a dream correctly, we need a thorough knowledge of the conscious situation at that moment, because the dream contains its unconscious complement, that is, the material which the conscious situation has constellated in the unconscious. Without this knowledge it is impossible to interpret a dream correctly, except by a lucky fluke."[9] Although the interpretations were interesting and plausible, there is no way to know if they were meaningful to the dreamer, who is the only one who can say whether an interpretation is on target.

The use of a dream dictionary to research the meaning of various symbols is an issue that frequently comes up when people begin to work with their dreams. While dictionaries have their place, they can never substitute for the dreamer's personal associations and meanings. Looking up symbols and images before putting in the time and effort necessary to figure out their meaning on a personal level ignores the unique nature of dreams and makes it unlikely that the dreamer will come to an understanding of what the psyche is trying to communicate. Dream dictionaries imply that symbols and images have fixed meanings (for example, a serpent equals sexuality; flying equals spirituality). Although Freud and others followed this school of thought, such an approach overlooks the individuality and uniqueness of each dreamer. C. G. Jung believed that there are universal symbols that are primordial or archetypal, that is, they are common to all human beings in all ages. Their meaning, however, is not fixed, but rather is determined by the dreamer's background and present circumstances. This implies that each of us has our own personal symbols that originate from emotionally charged experiences that recur throughout our lifetime. An identical dream, if dreamed by two dreamers, will not have identical meanings, but rather different meanings, each unique to the dreamer. This is why it is important to work on a dream without the aid of a dictionary first, and then turn to it as a resource for strange or new symbols or to supply additional associations to what we have come up with on our own.

THE PITFALL OF LITERAL INTERPRETATION

Another common mistake when working with dreams is moving too quickly to a literal interpretation. While dreams mean exactly what they say and say exactly what they mean, they speak the language of symbol and metaphor. There is a difference between the missing eyeglasses dream mentioned earlier, in which an image of glasses on a carpet is meant to be taken literally, and the following, more typical kind of dream that needs to understood on a symbolic level. This is the dream of a close friend, who telephoned the morning after having the dream because it was so disturbing. In the dream she is told that she has breast cancer. The dream wakes her up in a panic, and she is flooded with anxiety. As we talked about the dream, it became clear that there was some basis in reality for her concern because she had a history of suspicious cysts and calcifications and at the time of the dream was awaiting results of a follow-up mammogram. As she tearfully talked about the dream, fearful that the dream might be literally true, she made several important associations that eventually led to an alternative, symbolic interpretation. Her first association was to her many such experiences in the past, all of which had turned out fine. Nothing was different this time, and yet she was in a state of panic. So, why the dream, and what is the anxiety about?

Her next association was to her husband, whose first wife had died of breast cancer and who himself was undergoing tests for prostate cancer. She had not told him of the follow-up mammogram because she was afraid of overwhelming him. As she spoke of her concern for him, as well as her fear of losing him to cancer, her anxiety lessened. She could see that the dream, rather than diagnosing her with cancer, was literally "waking her up" to how her anxiety was growing out of control like a cancer. She was in such a state of paralysis that it had not occurred to her that she could call her doctor directly to get the results of her follow-up mammogram. Later that day, when she did so, she was reassured that the mammogram was negative. The impulse to interpret a dream literally seems greatest when the dream shows something we fear. Before we jump to any conclusions, it is important to be able to step back and evaluate it rationally. In this case there was something concrete that could be done to find out the results of the mammogram. This example also illustrates how valuable it is to have someone with whom we can share and process our dreams, especially when their impact is so powerful and arresting.

Another category of dreams that are vulnerable to literal interpretation are death dreams, when, for example, we dream that a loved one has died and awake believing that person is on his or her deathbed. In all probability the dream is using death as a metaphor. Something in the dreamer has died or needs to die; or, since death means separation from a loved one, the dream may also be suggesting that something is separating the dreamer from a loved one; or finally, it may mean that the dreamer needs to gain greater separation or independence.

An example of death as a metaphor occurred in a dream that Noreen had several months after the death of her father, in which she saw him in his coffin, coming back to life. In the dream she says, "Oh, no, we have to go through this all over again," a reference to the sad and painful experience she had shared with her family as they cared for him during his final illness. Upon waking, Noreen was reminded of a dream she had had five years earlier as she began Jungian analysis. In that dream she was wearing a very large pair of men's dress shoes, so large, in fact, that she could not keep them on her feet. On waking, she realized that the shoes were her father's size thirteen dress shoes. When she thought about her father, who was still living at the time, she realized how much she admired and even idealized him. To her, he was the perfect father and husband. This earlier dream called her attention to her identification with her father and suggested that she was not living her own life or walking in her own shoes. In the coffin dream after her father's death she realized that the inner work of becoming a separate and unique self is ongoing and that the death of her father did not mean the end of that sometimes painful struggle.

A death dream from a graduate student further illustrates the symbolic richness of dreams and how a person's openness to their message can initiate a healing process.

> *Dream:* About six months ago I had a dream that I can best describe as mind-boggling and a bit on the freakish side. I dreamed I was at my mom's funeral. The funeral was over, and the procession with the casket had gone down the aisle. I was walking down the aisle toward the back door when I looked down at someone sitting in the pew. It was my mom as a young woman, dressed in black, and mourning. She looked up at me and said, "'I miss you so much.'"

> *Dreamer's Response:* My mom is still alive (eighty-four years old), and my relationship with her is at best very

difficult. She has always been verbally and emotionally abusive to me and my family. I see her once a week. Her love is suffocating, and she always tells me she misses me so much. A friend of mine was instrumental in helping me understand my dream. He comes from the school of thought that the main character in any dream is ourselves. He told me that the woman dressed in black is me. The woman said she missed me. Jim told me that this was not my mom, but me as a young child.

I was mourning, not the person in the casket, but the young, loving mom that I, as a child and actually all my life, never had. I had never thought of this, but it is absolutely true. This dream revealed something about me that I could never have imagined. This reality came from my shadow side and just might help me deal with my mom in a loving way instead of out of anger. The question is this: "Can I stop being angry because I was not treated as I wanted or should have been treated? Can I finally stop hating her for what she probably could never give?" The other question that remains unanswered is why she makes me so angry in other ways. What is it in me that makes me so angry?

This student is new to dream-work, and yet we see how quickly he is able to grasp the significance of this dream and how he intuitively moves to challenging himself to take responsibility for dealing with his anger.

DEVALUING WHAT IS NEW IN A DREAM

The purpose of dreams is to enlarge our self-awareness, to give us information that is useful at this particular time in our life. Since each dream has a purpose, we can take it for granted that dreams are not telling us something we already know, although at first glance, it may seem this way. The best approach to take when we have a dream is to presume there is some new and timely message for us. This will avoid the mistaken notion that some dreams are "old news" or perhaps caused by something we ate for dinner. Jung strongly believed that we should approach each dream as something unknown to us.

HOW TO WORK WITH OUR DREAMS

In the following section there are some practical guidelines for working with dreams. There is no universally accepted formula for interpreting dreams, so we have chosen to introduce the approach that we have used with our own dreams and in facilitating dream-work with others.

1. Record the Dream

A dream journal is a good way to keep dreams together and organized in chronological order. Some people prefer a binder, as it allows pages to be added or removed; others find the spiral-bound notebook makes it easier when they travel. The type of notebook is less important than having a place for it next to our bed. It is essential that we record a dream as soon as we awake, before we forget it. When writing down a dream, we should include as many details as we can recall, including people, animals, smells, colors, sounds, feelings, emotions, and our mood upon awaking. The feelings of the characters in the dream are particularly important in dream interpretation, as is the atmosphere of the dream (ominous, barren, lighthearted, and so on). After recording the dream, date it and give it a title.

2. Record Your Associations to the Dream

What thoughts or memories does the dream evoke? It is also helpful to think back to the previous day and write down anything that stands out (for example, an unresolved argument with a friend, a feeling of failure at work, a persistent sad mood), so that as you are working on the dream, you can see if it relates to an issue or problem that surfaced that day.

3. What Story Is the Dream Telling?

Dreams are like a drama. They have a beginning (an opening scene that sets the stage or states the problem), a middle (the problem unfolds), and an end (sometimes a solution is hinted at; at other times, the dream ends with no resolution). This dramatic structure is an important aspect of the dream message and may indicate a causal relationship between scene I and scene II or between scenes II and III. Summarize the plot of your dream in a few steps, noting the sequence of events. Ask yourself, What in my life is like this story?

4. Personifications of the Dreamer

List and then describe each of the known characters in the dream. Briefly describe each of them. List the characters that are unknown to you, and note down your associations. Next, ask yourself if there is any way in which you are like each dream figure. If there are figures you cannot relate to at all, ask yourself if this could personify an unknown part of you. Repeat this exercise with each object or nonhuman image in the dream.

5. Outstanding Image

What is the outstanding image in the dream—earthquake, new house, orphaned child, wild animal? What feelings or emotions does the image evoke in you? How does this image relate to your life at the present time? When have you felt this way recently? Does this image symbolize previous times in your life?

6. Active Imagination

Continue the dream by developing the story. What happened next? If the dream did not have an ending, make up one. Is there a dream figure that remains unknown or a figure that stirs your curiosity? Engage that figure in an imaginative conversation so that you find out what part of you it personifies. Dreams that are frightening, like nightmares, can be addressed with this technique. If someone is breaking into your house in the dream, you can ask the intruder what he or she wants from you. Nightmares or recurring dreams usually mean that the dreamer is not paying attention to something important.

7. Live with the Dream

Since dreams are addressing our blind spots, it makes sense to presume that we will have some degree of resistance to their message. When we find that the step-by-step approach described above still leaves us in the dark, we can try living with the dream as we go about the next few days. By carrying dream images into daily life, pondering them at our leisure, perhaps drawing the image that most impresses us, we open ourselves to memories and connections that eluded us when we took a more focused approach. Because dream images are symbolic and always have multiple levels of meaning, dream interpretation is not a certain science.

More like a parable than a docudrama, any dream can have several messages.

8. Make an Interpretation

After working with a dream and making every effort we can to understand its images and symbols, we should attempt an interpretation. If the interpretation we make touches us on a feeling level, we know that we have understood at least part of the dream's message. Sometimes an interpretation makes sense on a rational level but does not move us on an emotional level. In this case the interpretation may not be wrong, but it is not likely to be the one that is relevant to our life right now. People whose job requires them to solve problems using their intellect, or those who by personality have a very rational approach to life, can become fascinated by their dreams and come up with great interpretations but remain emotionally unaffected. Success in understanding the messages from our deeper self is a matter of using the heart more than the head. It is always a good practice to think of our interpretations as tentative and to remain open to the possibility that a new dream may correct an interpretation that is off the mark, reemphasize a choice we must make, or validate one we have already made.

DISCERNMENT CONFIRMATION

The experience of a colleague illustrates the way in which a dream can confirm and support an important life decision. First, some background is necessary. After a long and painful discernment process, our colleague made the decision to separate from her husband of many years. His history of substance abuse and recent outbursts of physical violence caused her at times to fear for her safety and that of their young daughter. Shortly after reaching this life-changing decision, she had the following dream:

> My husband has gone away. No one knows where he is. My daughter finds him and tells me where he is. He is at a lake outside the town where I grew up. I go there. It is pitch black. I see my husband lying on a sarcopha-gus-like box with his hands folded over his chest, as though he's dead. He is asleep. I see him in this really dark place.

For the dreamer, this dream was a source of inner support and affirmed the decision she had reached. Because divorce was contrary to her religious belief in marriage as a sacred, unbreakable bond, she had been struggling with feelings of guilt and self-blame for ending her marriage. By presenting images of a husband who has gone away and lies in "pitch blackness" in a death-like sleep on a coffin-like box, the dream shows the condition of the dreamer's marriage. It says nothing about blame; it simply shows what her situation is in reality. That her inner child has led her to a place where she can see this calls to mind Isaiah's comment that "a little child shall lead them" (Isa 11:6). Often in dreams, as in fairy tales and myths, it is the child, the naive, innocent, undefended part of us, who leads the way or who sees reality as it is.

We should remember that the goal of inner work is to build a channel of communication between our waking self and our deeper self. The development and strengthening of this connection—which Jungian psychology calls the ego-Self axis—gives us the ability to tap into the wisdom and creativity of the psyche. Our growth in wholeness depends on this, so much so that psychological and spiritual maturity is impossible when there is no dialogue between ego and soul.

DISCERNING BY DAY AND BY NIGHT

Among the various gospel accounts of the sower and the seed, there is one that is often unnoticed because of its brevity. In four short verses Mark relates the story of a man who scatters seed on the land. Night and day, while he is asleep or awake, the seed is sprouting and growing; he does not know how. On its own the earth produces first the shoot, then the ear, then the full grain in the ear. When the crop is ripe, the sower at once starts to reap because the harvest has come (Mark 4:26–29). This parable presents a positive way of viewing the role of dreams in discernment. While dreams may not yield immediate answers or produce ready-made solutions to our quandaries, they nevertheless provide useful information that is invaluable in our discernment process. By allowing for the spontaneous emergence of information that has been out of the reach of our conscious mind, dreams can surprise us with rich insights that we can harvest and use in discernment. As we have discussed above, dreams can reveal to us blind spots that limit the view that our conscious mind possesses. Sometimes our blindness is due to an unwillingness to acknowledge certain realities in our life because we resist the possibility of change; denial preserves the status quo. Or sometimes dreams can help us break through viewing things in a habitual way that blinds us to new possibilities.

Dreams can powerfully alter our perception of our situation and reveal hopeful possibilities by creating a "gestalt shift." Gestalt psychology holds that we perceive things in patterns or configurations, that is, in terms of figure and ground or foreground and background. If either the figure or the ground shifts, we see something entirely different. The classic example is that of a picture that can be seen as either two faces looking at each other or as a vase, depending on the configuration. Dreams, especially big ones, have the capacity to change dramatically how we view the alternatives that are open to us and thus effect a liberating gestalt shift in our discernment process. Like the sower, we are sometimes mystified by the power and relevance of dreams in helping us with life choices and concerns. By staying open to the guidance of God that can come through dreams, we affirm our faith that our God is a God of light and a God of darkness, who supports us in our search "night and day," while we are asleep and while we are awake. Honoring the possible contribution of dreams to our discernment process is a way of broadening our view of how the illimitable mystery of God can touch us with support and guidance.

Dream Interpretation Guide

Date: _____

Title: _____

Dream (write it down):

Reflection:

1. What comes to mind (associations, memories, and so on)?
2. What feelings did you have in the dream? On waking?
3. What happened yesterday in your outer life? In your inner life?
4. Was the dream setting familiar? Have you been to a similar place? What does it remind you of? What was the feeling tone? When have you felt like this?
5. Story: Summarize the plot in a few chronological steps (first...then...and then...). What in your life is like this story?
6. Characters: List and then describe each of the known people in the dream. What is the outstanding characteristic of each? Describe each of the unknown people. What are the associations to each?
7. What part of you is each character personifying? Ask yourself if there is any way in which you are like that character. If you cannot relate at all to a dream figure, ask yourself if this might represent a rejected part of you.
8. What is the outstanding image (earthquake, fire, house, animal)? What are the feelings that this image evokes? Is there any aspect of your life that feels like this?
9. Continue the dream: Dialogue with dream figures that you wish to know more about. Find out why they are in your dream.

VII.
EMBRACING OUR
PERSONAL PATH

Thoroughly unprepared we take the step into the afternoon of life;
worse still, we take this step with the false presumption that our
truths and ideals will serve us as hitherto. But we cannot live the
afternoon of life according to the programme of life's morning—for
what was great in the morning will be little at evening, and what
in the morning was true will at evening become a lie.
    —C. G. Jung, *Modern Man in Search of a Soul*

Very truly, I tell you, when you were younger, you used to fasten
your own belt and to go wherever you wished. But when you
grow old, you will stretch out your hands, and someone else
will fasten a belt around you and take you where
you do not wish to go....Follow me.
    —John 21:18–19

As Christians we are all called to find and follow the particular direction and purpose God intends for us. This vocation or calling is "a gradual revelation—of me to myself by God. Over a lifetime I gradually learn the shape of my life. And it takes a lifetime."[1] When we are young, few of us could bear to know all the turns and detours of the journey ahead. To embrace life with enthusiasm and hope throughout its course—from our youth, through our middle years,

195

and into our senior years—requires ongoing shifts and profound changes, the revamping of earlier plans and adjustments to unforeseen events. Adaptation and change are necessary if we are to continue living with meaning and vitality. A faithful following of God requires that we stay in an ongoing conversation with the God of Easter, who always leads us from dead ends into new highways of possibilities, from deserts of desolation to oases of fresh hope.

In his spiritual classic *Poverty of Spirit* theologian Johannes Metz expresses a notion of our human vocation that is dynamic and lifelong. He states that being is entrusted to us "as a summons" that we must "accept and consciously acknowledge." Unlike other living things that are created with a completeness in their being from the first moment of their existence, human beings are challenged to grow into what it means to be human over the course of our lives. From the start we are unrealized potential. In the process of personal development we must win our selfhood and decide what we are to be through the exercise of our freedom. Because of the depths of our boundless spirit, we have an open-ended relationship with ourselves. Growth as self-transcendence entails the willingness to strive for "the more" that we can be tomorrow. By its very nature this process of freely becoming a human being is a trial and has built-in temptations. As Metz states:

> Man, entrusted with the task of making himself man, faces danger at every side. He is always a potential rebel. He can secretly betray the humanity entrusted to him....He can try to run away from himself, from the burdens and the difficulties of his lot, even going so far as to take his own life....He can "stifle" the truth of his being...thus aborting his work of becoming a human being.[2]

Growth as continual self-transcendence entails an ongoing process of death and rebirth. This daunting process fortunately finds biblical encouragement in Jesus' instruction to Nicodemus, who sought Jesus' guidance in his own discernment of a spiritual path (John 3:1–8). To be alive to the mystery of God's Spirit at work in our lives, we must, as Jesus made clear to Nicodemus, be willing to be born *anothen*. The Greek word used in the text is significant because it has a double meaning: "again and again" and "from above." The first meaning of the word reinforces the notion that ongoing human growth calls for periodic separations and losses that feel like "deaths" in order for new life or rebirth to occur. The second meaning of the word reassures us that God is intimately involved in these rebirths and that new life will come "from above."

A rabbinic story nicely complements Metz's understanding of the built-in challenge of becoming fully human. A rabbi once proposed a riddle that involved the creation account in chapter 1 of Genesis. The riddle went this way: After finishing work on each of the first five days, the Bible states, "God saw that it was good." But, God is not reported to have commented on the goodness of what was created on the sixth day, when the human person was fashioned. "What conclusion can you draw from that?" asked the rabbi. Someone volunteered, "We can conclude that the human person is not good." "Possibly," the rabbi nodded, "but that's not a likely explanation." He then went on to explain that the Hebrew word translated as "good" in Genesis is the word *tov*, which is better translated as "complete." That is why, the rabbi contended, God did not declare the human person to be *tov*. Human beings are created incomplete. It is our life's vocation to collaborate with our creator in fulfilling the Christ-potential in each of us. As the medieval mystic Meister Eckhart suggested, Christ longs to be born and developed into fullness in each of us. "What good is it to me if Mary gave birth to the son of God fourteen hundred years ago," Meister Eckhart once asked, "and I do not also give birth to the son of God in my time and in my culture?"[3]

THE WAY OF JESUS AND ONE'S PERSONAL PATH

To follow Jesus along the way that leads to holiness requires us to discover our personal path and pursue it faithfully. While being recommissioned by the risen Jesus at the Sea of Tiberias after his triple affirmation of love, Peter is momentarily distracted at the sight of John, the beloved disciple, following them and asks Jesus "What about him, Lord?" Jesus' response, in effect, was, "Peter, this is the path I have set for you. Never mind about John. If I want him to stay behind till I come, what does it matter to you? *You* are to follow me" (John 21:20–23, paraphrased). Throughout his life, Jesus modeled what he consistently taught to be the essence of discipleship: a deep resolve to do God's will, a receptivity to the Spirit of God directing one's movements, and an abiding trust that the ever-faithful God will always bring life from death, good from evil. His faith in God enabled him to pursue his particular path even in the face of persecution and powerlessness, rejection and betrayal. To imitate Christ today is to follow the movements of God as they unfold in the unique and particular pattern that shapes our personal path. As psychologist Josef Goldbrunner, applying depth psychology to spiritual development, asserts, "There is no universal way to perfection. The real starting point should be the individual. Authentic sanctity is always bound up with the *uniqueness,* with the limited talents and potentialities of the individual," which are his or her truth. "It is wrong to say: 'That is how I want to develop!'

What one should say is 'What does God expect from me and my particular talents?'"[4] The guiding voice of God may be mysteriously indistinct or inaudible at times. Yet the religious person perseveres in faith, for, as Michael Buckley affirms, one "who follows God moves into mystery without prematurely forcing clarity because his experience of God directs this movement."[5]

Fidelity to the path by which we are uniquely called to love in the world requires the same kind of inner freedom and courage that Jesus exhibited when he, despite ridicule and rejection, followed his call. A common obstacle for many of us who feel inspired to follow Jesus' resoluteness is the fear of what others are going to think of us. Freedom is gained when the need for human approval is defeated, as the following story told by Anthony de Mello illustrates:

> The Master seemed quite impervious to what people thought of him. When the disciples asked how he had attained this stage of inner freedom, he laughed aloud and said, "Till I was twenty I did not care what people thought of me. After twenty I worried endlessly about what my neighbors thought. Then one day after fifty I suddenly saw that they hardly ever thought of me at all!"[6]

Genuine imitation of Christ consists in following his example of deep devotion to God and unwavering pursuit of his vision of proclaiming the kingdom rather than simply imitating the external aspects of his life. Mere mindless imitation will get us nowhere on the spiritual path.

> After the Master attained Enlightenment, he took to living simply—because he found simple living to his taste.
> He laughed at his disciples when they took to simple living in imitation of him.

"Of what use is it to copy my behavior," he would
say, "without my motivation? Or to adopt my motivation without the vision that produced it?"

They understood him better when he said, "Does a
goat become a rabbi because he grows a beard?"[7]

Like Jesus, we too must stay in touch with our inner call and
the Spirit-inspired vision for our lives through prayerful discernment.

THE PROCESS OF INDIVIDUATION

Put in the language of Jungian psychology, pursuing our
personal path involves individuation, the process by which
we become ourselves, distinct from other people. We grow
in wholeness by becoming conscious of the shadow, Jung's
term for those parts of ourselves that are buried in the
unconsciousness. We become distinct from other people by
affirming our uniqueness as individuals. Psychologist
Lawrence Jaffe comments that many of his clients are "often
possessed by the uncontrollable desire to be what they call
normal, by which they generally mean just like everyone
else. They forget they were meant to be something unprece-
dented...a mystery that only they, with the help of God, can
realize by living their life...with the sincerity and devotion
that Christ lived his."[8]

Just as we were not mass produced, but rather created in
"lone nativities" by a God who counts every hair on our
head, we must each discern the unique ways we are called to
live out our life as an act of praise and gratitude to God. At
various points in our life—early adulthood, midlife, retirement—we find ourselves asking: How specifically am I being
called *now* to love God and others? Given my unique personality, talents, health, background, and experience, what

is my particular way of serving God and contributing to society? Only such questions can help us choose a personal way among a multiplicity of possible ways. Martin Buber makes this point in a story entitled "The Particular Way":

> Rabbi Baer of Radoshitz once said to his teacher the "Seer" of Lublin: "Show me one general way to the service of God." The zaddik replied: "It is impossible to tell men what way they should take. For one way to serve God is through learning, another through prayer, another through fasting, and still another through eating. Everyone should carefully observe what way his heart draws him to, and then choose this way with all his strength."[9]

As the zaddik of Buber's story observes, it is impossible to tell individuals what path they should take. Each person must discover his or her own way through a process of heart searching.

Mature discernment first requires that individuals take responsibility for their own lives. We are called to cast our cares upon the Lord, not our responsibility (1 Pet 5:7). Some people refuse to stand on their own two feet and, directly or indirectly, communicate the message, "Tell me what to do, how to live." This kind of dependence on others makes discernment impossible because it detracts from the serious attention that should be given to one's inner life, one's thoughts, feelings, values, aspirations, attractions, and repulsions. These inner realities make up the data that can eventually form the basis for a well-grounded decision. Turning one's glance inward in solitude provides access to the heart and the valuable data stored within.

The poet Rainer Maria Rilke's advice to a young man wondering whether he should be a poet reinforces the importance of intimate self-knowledge for those searching for direction in their lives:

> You ask whether your verses are good. You ask me. You have asked others before. You send them to magazines. You compare them with other poems, and you are disturbed when certain editors reject your efforts. Now...I beg you to give up all that. You are looking outward and that above all you should not do now. Nobody can counsel and help you, nobody. There is only one single way. Go into yourself. Search for the reason that bids you to write; find out whether it is spreading out its roots in the deepest places of your heart, acknowledge to yourself whether you would have to die if it were denied you to write. This above all—ask yourself in the stillest hour of your night: *must* I write? Delve into yourself for a deep answer. And if this should be affirmative, if you may meet this earnest question with a strong and simple *"I must,"* then build your life according to this necessity; your life even into its most indifferent and slightest hour must be a sign of this urge and a testimony to it.[10]

Both Rilke and Buber voice an inescapable fact of discernment: it entails a heart searching that each of us must do for ourself. Of course, feedback and advice from others are important. But they can neither supersede nor supplant the kind of self-intimacy that allows us to encounter the guiding presence of God within. If our questions are not tested and matured in solitude, it is unrealistic to expect answers that are really our own.

COMPANIONS ON THE JOURNEY

Because of the complex nature of choosing, the ideal context for discernment is conversational. Thus, we can understand the invaluable role of a trusted friend, pastor, spiritual director, or therapist. In this final chapter we want to share some of the ways that our work in spiritual direction and psychoanalysis has supported those discerning important life choices. Helping relationships in general, when characterized by empathic understanding, warmth, and respect, aid us in recognizing and honoring the movements of our inner life as we prayerfully seek indications of God's lead from within. They provide a safe container in which the unresolved questions of our heart are honored without fear of external judgment and interference. They provide a hospitable environment in which all our disparate desires and aspirations, feelings and concerns, hopes and fears can be tentatively expressed, mutually explored, and gently held until we become clear about how we are being led by the Spirit of God. In our work in spiritual direction and psychoanalysis, we appreciate how privileged we are. As Quaker Douglas V. Steere put it so eloquently, "To 'listen' another's soul into a condition of disclosure and discovery may be almost the greatest service that any human being ever performs for another."[11]

While psychoanalysis deals with the whole gamut of issues and concerns that people bring to therapy, the focus of a Jungian analyst has a distinctively spiritual quality. "There is something very special about the analytical experience," states Albert Kreinheder. "It is a unique kind of meeting whose purpose, whether articulated or not, is a holy one, having to do with the meaning of one's life; and behind such a question always lurks the mystery of that which we cannot see."[12] Beyond crisis management and

problem-solving, analysis entails a kind of "soul work" that
addresses the depth dimensions of human life:

> When we come to analysis, we must eventually face the
> ultimate questions, because it turns out that they are
> necessary in solving the lesser question for which we
> thought we came. If the therapist has the appropriate
> awe, then the patient too will sense that this is "soul
> work," and then the healing gods will come.[13]

Similarly, work in spiritual direction is essentially a ministry of accompaniment. Spiritual directors walk with others
who want assistance and support as they discern the lead of
God. A biblical illustration of how spiritual directors contribute to the discernment process is contained in the story
of the call of Samuel, which occurred when he lived with
the priest Eli in the Temple (1 Sam 3:1–14). In the stillness
of night Samuel hears his name being called three times.
Each time, Samuel mistakenly thinks it is Eli who is calling
him. Finally, it dawns on Eli that the voice addressing
Samuel is that of the Holy One. He then directs the young
Samuel to respond to the voice by saying, "Speak, Yahweh,
your servant is listening." Eli's help enabled Samuel to have
a religious experience from which his vocation as a prophet
emerged. Similarly, contemporary spiritual directors try to
listen to people's stories with contemplative ears, helping
them to detect where God is calling them and supporting
their movement to that place, all the while encouraging
them to pray with openness to be led. The human director's
role is purely instrumental and secondary: to help directees
get connected to the present promptings of the living God.
In a key instruction directed to retreat directors in the *Spiritual Exercises,* Ignatius states that God is ultimately the
Director of souls. Thus, Ignatius counsels, the human director should not get in the way and "should permit the Cre-

ator to deal directly with the creature, and the creature directly with his Creator and Lord" (no. 15).

SUPPORT IN THE "NOT KNOWING" ZONE OF LIMINAL SPACE

Spiritual directors and therapists help us "stay with" our process as we enter into that anxious place of "not knowing," that in-between time when the known and familiar have passed and the new has not yet come into being. This transition phase is commonly referred to as *liminality,* a term taken from anthropologist Victor Turner's study of initiation rites or rites of passage.[14] In primitive and traditional societies transition periods are facilitated and marked by rites of passages. These rites mark such transitions as the movement from childhood into adolescence, from adolescence into adulthood, from single to married status, from non-parenthood to parenthood, and from this life to the life beyond. These rites attempt to move individuals through life transitions and to make these transitions actually transformative.[15]

The transitions consist of three phases: separation, liminality, and reincorporation. In the first phase initiants are ritually separated from the social group that until then defined their cultural roles and identities and removed to a secluded place. The novitiate process in the initial formation of Catholic priests and religious parallels this first stage of separation, especially when novitiates and seminaries are located in remote and isolated locations. Removal from society inaugurates the second phase of initiation, the liminal phase. The goal of the liminal phase is to bring about a personal transformation that enables people to redefine who they are and to reorient their lives in terms of this new identity and consciousness. When the liminal phase is completed, reincorporation rites signal their re-entry into the social group as a "new" person.

This anthropological description of initiation rites provides a helpful framework for understanding psychological and spiritual growth, which entails a series of endings (separation), transitions (liminality), and new beginnings (reincorporation). The pattern of developmental growth requires moving from stage to stage. To grow we have to leave one stage in order to enter into another. For example, at certain pivotal points in life we have to let go of a familiar way of understanding who we are in order to acquire a new psychological identity that allows us to incorporate new aspects of the self that long to be lived out in us. We human beings, like puzzles, are made up of many parts. Our self-concept allows us to experience ourselves as a single entity rather than as a loose collection of unrelated parts. However, unlike prefabricated puzzles with limited parts, we are multifaceted beings whose many dimensions are only discovered over the course of a lifetime.

When new aspects of our self emerge at different points in our life's journey, growth in wholeness requires that they be recognized and given their rightful place. Integrating these aspects often requires that we allow a restrictive self-concept to dissolve so that a more complex one, capable of incorporating these newly discovered parts, can emerge. This dissolution provokes anxiety because it changes our sense of who we are, often precipitating an identity crisis and creating momentary disequilibrium. There are times when this process is experienced as a breakdown and, in a sense, it is, because the old self has to die for a new self to be born. It is natural to want to cling to the old, even when it is no longer meaningful, because at least it is familiar. Spiritual and psychological growth, however, requires letting go of our confining and narrow self-images and risking becoming more than we think we are.

In midlife the challenge is to cultivate those aspects of the personality that have remained latent and under-developed due to their neglect during the first half of our life. Thus, the midlife project requires looking at and owning our shadow (aspects of the self that were earlier repressed) and growing androgynously through the progressive assimilation of the feminine *(anima)* and masculine *(animus)* principles in the development of our personality. This midlife transition amounts to the birth of a new self, which requires the "death" of the former self. Such a transition, especially when it is acutely painful, can be greatly helped by analysis. Jungian analysts Jan and Murray Stein describe the role of the analyst in the following way:

> What we judge to be the most fitting attitude for therapeutic intervention during the midlife transition is indicated by the term "maieutic." "Maieutics" refers to the science and art of midwifery, of attending to the process of giving birth. Since the person in midlife transition is ultimately birthing a new self, the goal of the psychotherapy is to facilitate this process. Psychological maieutics, then, is the science and art of facilitating the psychic transformation and the emergence of new psychological structures.... This is done by "containing" affect and behavior that derive from inner changes; a flexible yet firm attitude of tolerance and understanding is called for, and some encouragement to continue coping with everyday matters and ego demands as much as reasonably possible.[16]

Spiritual direction, on the other hand, supports life transitions by reminding us of the paschal pattern of all growth, that is, that new life can only come through death. This is the crux of Christian faith and is based on Jesus' solemn pronouncement that "unless a grain of wheat falls into the earth and dies, it remains just a single grain; but if it dies, it bears much fruit" (John 12:24).

THE IMPORTANCE OF LIMINAL SPACE IN DISCERNMENT

The gap created by the dissolution of the old and the yet-to-emerge new is what we are calling liminal space. It is a place of disequilibrium. Visually, it can be pictured as the moment when the trapeze performer lets go of one bar and waits in midair to connect with another. In life transitions, however, this analogy limps because the connecting bar does not suddenly appear but must be discovered through a process of discernment. Nevertheless, liminality is like hanging in midair until it becomes clear to us what we are to grab. A place where we are caught betwixt and between, liminal space is psychologically and spiritually significant because it is where real transformation can take place. Describing liminal space as "a narrow place without answers," Richard Rohr insists on the importance of liminal space for spiritual growth:

> Nothing new happens as long as we are inside our self-constructed comfort zone. Nothing good or creative emerges from business as usual. Much of the work of the God of the Bible is to get people into liminal space, and to keep them there long enough so they can learn something essential. It is the ultimate teachable space, maybe the only one.[17]

Spiritual directors and psychotherapists can contribute to the work of God by helping us tolerate the insecurity of not knowing until we discover what God wants us to learn.

Few of us know how to inhabit liminal space. "If we are security-needy by temperament," comments Rohr, "we will always run back to the old room that we have already constructed. If we are risk-taking by temperament, we will quickly run to a new room of our own making and liking. Hardly anyone wants to stay on the threshold 'without answers.'"[18] From a purely philosophical point of view, we know that the willingness to accept temporary uncertainty is an important aspect of sound thinking and problem-solving. Linking the tolerance of uncertainty to reflective thinking, John Dewey, the famous American pragmatist, states:

> Reflective thought involves an initial state of doubt or perplexity....To many persons both suspense of judgment and intellectual search are disagreeable; they want to get them ended as soon as possible....To be genuinely thoughtful, we must be willing to sustain and protract the state of doubt, which is the stimulus to thorough inquiry.[19]

Like reflective thought, sound discernment is also thwarted by hasty decisions and compulsive quick fixes. "Some people will never learn anything," states Jesuit Anthony de Mello, "because they grasp too soon. Wisdom, after all, is not a station you arrive at, but a manner of traveling....To know exactly where you're headed may be the best way to go astray. Not all who loiter are lost."[20]

Christian spirituality encourages us to stay with liminal space by reassuring us that God is present and active during these fearful times of disorientation. Anxious about not being in control or having a clear direction for our life, we are often tempted to seek a quick reordering in order to take away our anxiety. We resist liminality, thinking despairingly that it is a meaningless abyss devoid of God's presence.

Christian tradition, however, is replete with symbols and illustrations of liminal space as an essential phase of spiritual growth, a period of divine purification, fruitful waiting, and inner preparation for something that God has in store for us. Recalling some of these illustrations can highlight the sacred dimension of liminality without denying the suffering that accompanies it:

- The wandering of the Israelites in the wilderness following their release from bondage in Egypt. The revelation of Exodus is that God was not only the Liberator who freed the captives, but also the Faithful One who guided them as a column of fire and a pillar of clouds in their frightening passage through the wilderness into the Promised Land.
- The time of Exile when the Jews had to wait patiently for the fulfillment of God's promise: "For thus says the LORD: Only when Babylon's seventy years are completed will I visit you, and I will fulfill to you my promise and bring you back to this place. For surely I know the plans I have for you, says the LORD, plans for your welfare and not for harm, to give you a future with hope. Then when you call upon me and come and pray to me, I will hear you" (Jer 29:10–12).
- The time in the tomb—for Lazarus and for Jesus—that issued forth in new life.
- The period of withdrawal that Saul of Tarsus spent in the desert of Arabia (Gal 1:7) following the sudden collapse of his career as a fire-breathing persecutor of the early Christians. His post-conversion experience in the desert provided the liminal space in which the Saul of old could be transformed into Paul, the great disciple to the Gentiles.

- Ignatius of Loyola's period of recuperation from the cannonball wound that not only shattered his knees but also his romantic dream of being a chivalrous knight in the service of a noble lady. Failure and suffering created the liminal space in which Ignatius discerned a new call in life that arose from the ashes of his defeat. Paying attention to the affective aftermath of his daydreams as he endured hours of healing, Ignatius was led to abandon his initial goals and worldly ambitions in order to serve Christ the King under the banner of the cross instead.
- The symbol of the dark night of Carmelite spirituality also conveys the deep transformation that often takes place in liminality when God works imperceptibly in darkness to purify and expand our capacity to love and to receive love.
- The forty days that Jesus spent in the wilderness (Luke 4:1–13; Matt 4:1–11; Mark 1:12–13) following his religious experience at his baptism in the Jordan, when he experienced profoundly that he was God's Beloved. In this liminal space prior to the inauguration of his public ministry, Jesus was both tempted by the devil and taught by the Spirit that led him there.

These examples indicate some of the reasons why liminality is such a spiritually fruitful space. In liminality we incubate the future. To incubate is to imitate the care of a mother hen, whose bodily warmth fosters embryonic development and hatches new life from eggs. To incubate is also to maintain optimal conditions for the development of new life. The historic careers of Saint Paul and Saint Ignatius of Loyola, for example, were hatched in liminal space. As in both their cases, failure and collapse can crack open a greater willingness in us to listen and to be led by God, which is the heart of discernment. When we feel we are in control, we are often close-minded in our pursuits. Pride and ambition deafen us to God's voice. However, when disruptions and crises throw us off track and we lose our way in life, we recognize that we are indeed poor in spirit and dependent on God for guidance.

Liminal space also provides the time we need to assimilate our religious experiences, especially when they are strong and intense, such as Saul's encounter of the risen Jesus on the road to Damascus and Jesus' profound experience of being addressed by God as the beloved Son. Peak religious experiences such as these need to be held in our hearts until we understand what they portend for our life and future. Thus, we must learn how to stay in liminal space. Sometimes we will need the support of spiritual direction and/or psychotherapy to keep us from running away, to reassure us that we are not in a useless place, and finally to curb our impulse to relieve our anxiety with a premature solution.

GOD'S ACTIVE PRESENCE IN LIMINAL SPACE

Liminal space often seems a lonely and dark place; yet Christian faith insists that our God is present, though imperceptibly, even in darkness. "Surely the LORD is in this place—and I did not know it!" (Gen 28:16). These words burst from Jacob's lips as he woke from a dream-filled sleep. Overnight, he felt his situation change dramatically. In a vivid dream that flooded him with fresh hope, he heard God say to him: "Jacob, the deal is still on. You don't have to worry; everything is still right between us. I will continue to honor the covenant I have with you and bless you with property and posterity. Be assured that I am with you and will keep you safe wherever you go; I will never desert you nor fail to come through for you as I promised" (Gen 28:13–15, paraphrased).

What a reassuring message for Jacob, caught in the darkness of liminality, in the middle of a family crisis that he had brought upon himself by stealing the blessing that rightfully belonged to his brother, Esau, as the firstborn. Already he was paying for what he had done by having to leave home in a hurry to escape Esau's murderous rage. Fortunately Rebekah, his quick-thinking mother, came to his rescue and sent him off to find refuge with her family in a far-off land. Safe for the moment, Jacob was still left with fears about his uncertain future. So the dream's message brought much relief to him as he struggled to deal with the sudden upheaval in his life. He had the strength to keep going because he believed that even in this dark place God was present. "How awesome is this place! This is none other than the house of God, and this is the gate of heaven!" (Gen 28:17).

Jacob's discovery that "the LORD is in this place—and I did not know it" challenges us to be more mindful of God's presence in times of painful transition, when we experience turmoil, fear, and loss. Jewish commentators have offered a couple of fruitful variant translations of Jacob's reaction to his revelatory dream. According to Rabbi Lawrence Kushner, one commentator offers a grammatical interpretation that supports translating the verse as: "Wow, God was in this place, but because of my 'I,' I did not know it!" The "I" that got in the way of Jacob's awareness of God, states Kushner, is the self-preoccupied ego or the distracting voice of self-consciousness that blocks full attention to present reality. Yet another variant translation would have Jacob crying out: "Wow, if I had known that God was in this place, I would not have gone to sleep." From this, Kushner concludes that we, like Jacob, often miss perceiving the presence of God because we are caught dozing![21] The irony, however, is that God's encouraging lead is available to us whether we are awake or asleep. We can "stay with" scary times of transition and honor the fruitfulness of liminal space, only if we, like Jacob, wake up to the realization that God has not deserted us and is present in the tough-going passages of our lives.

LIMINAL SPACE AND SELF-KNOWLEDGE

Liminal space provides the opportunity to grow in self-knowledge. Such, it seems, was the experience of Jesus in his liminal experience in the desert. The gospel accounts (Matt 4:1–11; Mark 1:12–13; Luke 4:1–13) dramatically set forth Jesus' struggle with temptations when "he was with wild beasts, and the angels looked after him" (Mark 1:13). The three temptations used by the devil had the single objective of luring Jesus away from the path of faithful obedience to God and total trust in God's power to help him accomplish his mission. Specifically, the first temptation prompted Jesus to establish his credentials as the Son of God through a display of power—by turning stones into loaves of bread. The second temptation urged him to accomplish his goals through panache by hurling himself over the parapet of the Temple. Finally, the third temptation tried to lure his allegiance away from God with a bribe that offered worldly riches and splendor.

From the point of view of a low Christology, which emphasizes the humanity of Jesus, it is interesting to speculate about Jesus' liminal experience in the desert. It has been suggested, for example, that the three temptations described were not confined to his forty days in the desert but illustrated what Jesus may have struggled with throughout his public ministry. Taken as a whole, these accounts can be seen as a literary expression of temptations that Jesus experienced regularly: to rely on power and worldly status to accomplish his mission rather than to depend on the power and reliability of God. Perhaps his intense struggle with these personal vulnerabilities in the desert etched in his soul lessons important for his personal discernment when making choices throughout his public ministry.

This interpretation helps to clarify, for example, Jesus' seeming overreaction to Peter, who pleaded in protest when Jesus predicted his passion, death, and resurrection (Mark 8:31–33). To hear Jesus say "Get behind me, Satan!" to his close friend Peter can be jarring. However, Jesus' sharp, immediate rebuke of Peter is understandable when we see that the devil's temptation of Jesus in the desert was now being unwittingly embodied in Peter's objection. Peter's rejection of the path of humility, suffering, and death may have touched off Jesus' own human ambivalence. Perhaps, knowing his own vulnerability, Jesus had to dismiss the danger at once.

When this Markan passage is interpreted this way, it provides a useful biblical basis for two Ignatian guidelines for dealing with temptation: boldness in rejecting temptation, and knowledge of our weakness. In his contemporary rendition of the *Spiritual Exercises,* Jesuit David Fleming expresses the first guideline as follows:

> The evil spirit often behaves like a spoiled child. If a person is firm with children, children give up petulant ways of acting. But if a person shows indulgence or weakness in any way, children are merciless in trying to get what they want, stomping their feet in defiance or wheedling their way into favor. So our tactics must include firmness in dealing with the evil spirit in our lives. [no. 325][22]

In the second guideline Ignatius states that "the enemy of human nature" is like a military commander who will attack us where we are weakest. Here Ignatius encourages a life stance of perceptive self-knowledge, especially regarding our personal vulnerabilities (no. 327). Acknowledging areas of our lives where we are most susceptible to temptation reflects a humility that recognizes and accepts all that we are.

Jesus' liminal experience in the desert also gave him the space to assimilate his profound experience of God at his baptism. In the Jordan, Jesus was struck by grace when the voice of the Creator of the universe proclaimed him to be the Beloved, always delightful in God's eyes. This core religious experience rooted his identity and shaped his intimate relationship with Abba, the Aramaic term that Jesus used to address God. *Abba* is best translated in familiar, intimate terms as "daddy" or "papa." Perhaps what fortified him in the face of hardship was his vivid memory, renewed regularly during all-night periods of prayer on the mountaintop, that he was indeed the Beloved in whom God took great delight.

It is interesting to see that after a narrow escape from a perilous encounter with his opponents, who "took up stones again to stone him" and "tried to arrest him," Jesus immediately "went again across the Jordan to the place where John had been baptizing earlier, and he remained there" (John 10:31–42). This allusion to his baptism suggests that Jesus' experience of God's loving affirmation in the River Jordan was the peak religious experience to which he returned whenever he needed divine reassurance and nurturance. These speculations would suggest that his liminal experience in the desert taught him not only the pattern of temptation in his life, but also the pattern of grace.

Liminal space provides us with the important opportunity to encounter our demons and angels. Because discernment as a human process is not infallible, we must, like Jesus, honor our own religious history and recognize both the pattern of temptation and the pattern of grace in our lives, that is, the personal ways we are susceptible to being deceived and misled as well as the peculiar ways in which we are influenced and led by the Divine. Jesuit William Barry states: "Discernment requires that I believe that God will show himself in my experience and that I yet be wary of mindless credulity toward that same experience." In the end, discernment is based, in Barry's words, on "two equally difficult and seemingly incompatible attitudes: to trust myself and my reactions and to recognize how easily I can delude myself."[23]

CHOOSING LIFE IN THE FACE OF FEAR

To live vibrant lives as Christians we must observe faithfully Moses' exhortation "to choose life" each day (Deut 30:19–20). A discerning heart enables us to scan the horizon of our lives and to choose those options that are enlivening and to avoid those that are stifling. We must have the courage to choose what most contributes to a life of love and vitality. Discerning life choices, like any other form of problem-solving, requires the courage to learn from mistakes and to live with uncertainty. As educational psychologist Michael Martinez put it, "Even if success is achieved, it will not be found by following an unerring path. The possibilities of failure and of making less-than-optimal moves are inseparable from problem-solving. And the loftier the goals, the more obvious will be the imperfection of the path toward a solution."[24] Courage is necessary because life-promising change often triggers fears that can choke off desire and choice. Spiritual directors and psychotherapists recognize these voices of fear in many who contemplate a serious life change:

- I don't feel up for it. I'm afraid of failing. What if I don't get the job? What if I don't get accepted into the program? What if he or she leaves me?
- What if my family and friends write me off as someone who's lost it, because they don't value my desires or agree with my hopes? What if they think I can't do it?
- What if the critics pan my work?
- Who am I to want this?
- Is a truly loving, sexual relationship possible for me with all my hang-ups about sex, intimacy, and trust due to being sexually abused when I was young?
- Do I have what it takes to be ordained?

Such inhibiting voices of fear, shame, and self-doubt are not new; we can hear them in Moses' response to God's call:

> But Moses said to God, "Who am I that I should go to Pharaoh, and bring the Israelites out of Egypt?" He said, "I will be with you." (Exod 3:11–12)
> Then Moses answered, "But suppose they do not believe me or listen to me, but say, 'The LORD did not appear to you.'" (Exod 4:1)

> But Moses said to the LORD, "O my Lord, I have never been eloquent, neither in the past nor even now that you have spoken to your servant; but I am slow of speech and slow of tongue." Then the LORD said to him, "Who gives speech to mortals? Who makes them mute or deaf, seeing or blind? Is it not I, the LORD? Now go, and I will be with your mouth and teach you what you are to speak." (Exod 4:10–12)
> "But he said, "O my Lord, please send someone else." (Exod 4:13)

We who struggle to choose life in the face of our fears can find much comfort in the response of the great leader

Moses, through whom God revealed the marvelous compassion of God for human suffering and those in bondage. Responding faithfully to God's call in our life does not mean never being afraid. What it does entail, however, is that we face and understand our fears as we discern our path. Because anxiety is a spoiler in the discernment process, we must not let anxiety possess us. Pastoral theologian Leroy Howe maintains that Christian caregivers help greatly when their ministry of presence provides people with a comforting relationship that enables them "to explore anew the roots of their fears, and what can be done to make things better for themselves and others."[25]

In addition to providing a "safe container" in which people can deal constructively with their fears, spiritual companions encourage them to bring those fears to prayer. The following is the account of a man overcome by anxiety about a new job who did just that:

> I chose to move on to my meditation...the "Stilling of the Storm" stories in the Gospels. I placed myself on the rugged boat among the other disciples and felt the fear well up when Jesus said we must leave the shore for the other side. I realized leaving my job was a huge leap but seem to have only felt the impact of that decision recently. I felt excited about being on the other shore but knew the trip to the other side might be frightful. Noticing my fear as we continued to sail, Jesus asked me, "What is it that you fear?" I found myself reciting a list:
>
> - What if I wasn't free, as Ignatius asks of us before making a decision?
> - What if I'm not smart enough or articulate enough for this job?
> - With all the required travel, how is this job going to affect my important relationships? Will they survive?

- Will the environment be more businesslike and competitive and conniving?
- Do I really have something to contribute?
- What if it doesn't work out and I'm out of a job again?

Jesus seemed to nod as he listened to my concerns, and then he said, "Do not be afraid," with a smile that comforted me because of the confidence it contained. He then asked me to take my fears, these statements and all those running through my mind, and dump them over the side of the boat and, in so doing, to release them to the waters. I proceeded to do this and felt some sense of letting go as I did so. Jesus raised his arms, and the waters calmed to the clear, still waters I had first imagined in my meditation. Instead of feeling completely calm, though, I still had some fear, which Jesus noticed. Instead of rebuking me for lack of faith, as he did the disciples in the scriptures, he simply said we would continue to dump the fears overboard until they had dissipated.

Clearly, the bringing of our concerns and fears to prayer does not magically take them away. It does, however, remind us that Jesus is "in the boat" with us, reassuring us that we will make it to the other side.

When we face the fears that confront us in discernment, we need to distinguish between realistic fears and imaginary fears. The former are based in reality; the latter are far-fetched. Because we cannot control all the possible outcomes of our choices, risk is always an element of discernment. Healthy fear motivates us to consider seriously the possible consequences of our choices and to evaluate the less than desirable consequences that may result. The fear response built into human nature heightens our awareness and makes us cautious in the face of danger. As such, it is a healthy instinct. However, the fear that flows from imagined dangers can consume us with anxious "what ifs" that can paralyze us into inaction. When anxieties are allowed to run wild, we lose our perspective on reality. We "what if" ourselves until our fear becomes debilitating.

A certain number of "what ifs" arise naturally from a realistic awareness of our vulnerability as human beings. For example, none of us, no matter how much wealth or power we possess, can guarantee that we will be unharmed by such things as natural disasters, cancerous cells, random accidents, terrorist violence, and human malice. Given this basic human vulnerability, it is understandable that we sometimes find ourselves caught up in catastrophic fear. Realistically, we know that these things can happen. Our Christian faith, however, encourages us to move through our fears, not denying them, but not allowing them to immobilize us. It calls us to remember that when we encounter difficulties and dangers, we are not alone. Ours is a lively faith that trustingly prays,

> Even though I walk through the darkest valley,
> I fear no evil;
> for you are with me;
> your rod and your staff—
> they comfort me. (Ps 23:4)

Philosopher John Macmurray contends that "All religion...is concerned to overcome fear." Real and illusory religion, however, can be distinguished "by contrasting their formulae for dealing with negative motivation." He continues:

> The maxim of illusory religion runs: "Fear not; trust in God and he will see that none of the things you fear will happen to you"; that of real religion, on the contrary, is "fear not; the things that you are afraid of are

quite likely to happen to you, but they are nothing to be afraid of."[26]

If our choices at times lead us into a dark valley, God will be there to guide and protect us. In discernment it is best to regard anxious "what ifs" as bad spirits that keep us from living with hope and enthusiasm. A student in the midst of discerning a major decision wrote:

> There is so much noise around me; some of it is my own head....I keep thinking about all the decisions that are on my immediate plate. Not all carry lifelong consequences. I don't feel the same turmoil I was feeling last week. I have a greater sense of peace now that I decided to focus on the "what is" rather than the "what ifs."

This peaceful insight reminds us that sound discernment is based on "what is," that is, what is rooted in reality. An incarnational faith invites us to discover the guiding and sustaining presence of God in the fleshy reality of our existence.

Patient Trust Needed in Discernment

Words of wisdom about the necessity of patient trust in the process of discernment come from the pen of three eloquent writers. The poet Rainer Maria Rilke advises the impatient seeker to

> be patient towards all that is unsolved in your heart and try to love the questions themselves. Do not seek the answers which cannot be given you because you would not be able to live them and the point is, to live everything. Live the questions now. Perhaps you will

gradually, without noticing it live along some distant
day into the answer.[27]

In a similar vein, Jesuit mystic and paleontologist Pierre
Teilhard de Chardin encourages us to be patient in times of
confusion and insecurity, when the path before us lies in
obscurity:

> Above all, trust in the slow work of God
> We are quite naturally impatient in everything
>   to reach the end without delay.
> We should like to skip the intermediate stages.
> We are impatient of being on the way to something
>   unknown, something new.
> And yet it is the law of all progress
>   that it is made by passing through
>   some stages of instability—
>   and that it may take a very long time.
>
> And so I think it is with you.
>   your ideas mature gradually—let them grow,
>   let them shape themselves without
>   undue haste.
> Don't try to force them on,
>   as though you could be today what time
>   (that is to say, grace and circumstances
>   acting on your own good will)
>   will make of you tomorrow.
>
> Only God could say what this new spirit
>   gradually forming within you will be.
> Give Our Lord the benefit of believing
>   that his hand is leading you,
> and accept the anxiety of feeling yourself
>   in suspense and incomplete.[28]

Because life provides no such thing as a crash course on detecting the ways of the Spirit, fashioning a discerning heart takes time. After more than half a century of striving to live attuned to the Spirit, retired Methodist bishop and author Rueben Job concludes:

> That God can be trusted may be the greatest learning of my life. When I remember that, I am much more likely to wait patiently and prayerfully for the revealing of God's will and the application of God's transforming power. This does not absolve me from the search for truth, the hard work of arriving at right decisions, and the price of costly action. But it does give me the assurance I need to wait, watch, listen, and expect an answer to the question around which I am seeking discernment. More often than not I am urged to begin taking steps toward the answer to the question for which I seek light and guidance.[29]

Epilogue
A MATTER OF
SEARCHING AND FINDING

IN THE END, OUR DISCERNMENT can be done lightheartedly because of faith's reassurance that God supports us in our search and is also simultaneously searching for us. In Matthew's Gospel we are encouraged to discern with hope and confidence: "Ask, and it will be given to you; search, and you will find; knock and the door will be opened to you" (7:7–8). This reassurance is based on God's unfathomable love for us, a love that far surpasses even our most cherished experiences of human love (7:11). God's unfathomable love for us moves God to search for us like a good shepherd who has lost a beloved sheep (Luke 15:4–7) and like a woman who has lost a precious coin (Luke 15:8–10). Both these stories in Luke's "lost and found" department highlight how unfathomable God's love actually is.

The story of the good shepherd starts off with a question that flies in the face of common sense: "Which one of you, having a hundred sheep and losing one of them, does not leave the ninety-nine in the wilderness and go after the one that is lost until he finds it?" (Luke 15:4). Even without having taken Business 101, we know that the most sensible thing for us to do in such a situation is to cut our losses by taking steps that will keep us from losing any more sheep, perhaps building better fences. It defies common sense to abandon the ninety-nine in search of the one. In the story of the lost coin we get a picture of God as a woman who combs all of creation in search of us, who are like precious coins that have been lost. While we sometimes do not deem ourselves as precious, we are always so in God's eyes. These stories convey the unfathomable nature of God's love for us. Discernment reveals our desire to find God in all our choices. Yet, even in our very desire to find God, God is already present. As Evelyn Underhill puts it, God is like one "who stoops toward [us] and first incites, and then supports and responds to [our] seeking."[1]

NOTES

Introduction

1. Michael J. O'Sullivan, "Trust Your Feelings, But Use Your Head: Discernment and the Psychology of Decision Making," *Studies in the Spirituality of Jesuits* 22, no. 4 (September 1990): 35.

2. Katherine Dyckman, Mary Garvin, Elizabeth Liebert, *The Spiritual Exercises Reclaimed: Uncovering Liberating Possibilities for Women* (Mahwah, NJ: Paulist Press, 2001), 327.

3. Henri Nouwen, *Reaching Out: The Three Movements of the Spiritual Life* (Garden City, NY: Doubleday, 1975), 27.

4. J. Jon Bruno, Los Angeles Episcopal Bishop, in a pastoral letter challenging the claims of "biblical orthodox" believers that the Episcopal Church has fallen from the faith by making official decisions that seem to be counter to the authority of Scripture, in *The Los Angeles Times*, August 23, 2004, B7. For a lucid explanation of two quite different ways of viewing Christian tradition and understanding the nature of biblical authority, see Marcus J. Borg, *The Heart of Christianity: Rediscovering a Life of Faith* (New York: HarperCollins, 2004).

5. Brian O'Leary, SJ, "Discernment and Decision-Making," *Review for Religious* (January-February 1992): 57.

6. This story was told by Madeleine L'Engle in a lecture entitled "100,000 Names of God," as part of the Staley Lectures at Bethel College, St. Paul, Minnesota, in April 1978.

I. The Discerning Heart

1. George Herbert, "God's Pulley," quoted in Robert F. Morneau, *Ashes to Easter: Lenten Meditations* (New York: Crossroad, 1997), 30–31.

2. Marcus Borg, *The Heart of Christianity: Rediscovering a Life of Faith* (New York: HarperCollins, 2004), 73.

3. Nancy Reeves, *I'd Say Yes, God, If I Knew What You Wanted* (Kelowna, British Columbia: Northstone Publishing, 2001), 209.

4. Paul Mariani, *Thirty Days: On Retreat with the Exercises of St. Ignatius* (New York: Penguin Putnam, 2002), 14–15.

5. Ibid., 29.

6. Ibid., 39.

7. Ibid., 174.

8. Douglas Burton-Christie, "Wisdom: The Hidden Face of God," *Weavings: A Journal of the Christian Spiritual Life* 17, no. 43 (July-August 2002): 8.

9. Ibid., 9.

10. James D. Whitehead and Evelyn Eaton Whitehead, *Shadows of the Heart: A Spirituality of Painful Emotions* (New York: Crossroad, 1996), 2.

11. Henry David Thoreau, "Economy," in *The Variorum Walden* (New York: Twayne Publishers, 1962), 28–29.

12. Evelyn Eaton Whitehead and James D. Whitehead, *Seasons of Strength* (Winona, MN: St. Mary's Press, 1995), 84.

13. Alan Watts, *Tao: The Watercourse Way* (New York: Pantheon Books/Random House, 1975), 76.

14. Gunilla Norris, "Many Ways: Fasting towards Self-Simplification," *Weavings: A Journal of Christian Spiritual Life* 19, no. 5 (September-October 2004): 9.

15. Watts, *Tao,* 76.

16. Thomas Merton, *The Way of Chuang Tzu* (New York: New Dimensions, 1969), 44.

17. Lao-tzu, quoted in Watts, *Tao,* 75,

18. Merton, *The Way of Chuang Tzu,* 45–47.

19. Reeves, *I'd Say Yes, God, If I Knew What You Wanted,* 63.

20. Ibid., 62.

21. Cf. Ignatius of Loyola, *Spiritual Exercises,* no. 236.

22. Borg, *The Heart of Christianity,* 31.

23. Ibid.

24. Teilhard de Chardin, "My Lord and My God," in *Hearts on Fire: Praying with Jesuits,* ed. Michael Harter, SJ (St. Louis: The Institute of Jesuit Sources, 1993), 80.

25. Ernest Larkin, OCarm., *Silent Presence: Discernment as Process and Problem* (Denville, NJ: Dimension Books, 1981), 16.

26. A more precise understanding of "consolation" and "desolation" in the *Spiritual Exercises* entails distinguishing between two groups of people: those in the purgative way, who are tempted "grossly and openly" (no. 9), and those in the illuminative way, who are tempted more subtly "under the appearance of good" (no. 10). For those who are tempted blatantly and are struggling to center their lives on God, consolation and desolation are properly understood more in terms of *directionality* than affectivity. In other words, whatever moves them *toward* God is considered to be consolation, no matter what feelings accompany that movement; conversely, whatever moves them *away* from God is considered to be desolation, irrespective of accompanying feelings. On the other hand, for those whose lives are already oriented toward God and who are tempted subtly by an apparent good (that is, evil under the guise of good), consolation and desolation are understood in terms of the *feelings that accompany their choices*. Here, consolation resembles the fruit of the Spirit delineated by Paul in his Letter to the Galatians (5:22–23). Desolation, on the other hand, includes feelings of disturbance, unrest, agitation, hopelessness, sadness, and so forth. Ignatius insists that it is critical for the spiritual director to recognize how a person is being tempted so that the appropriate guidelines for the discernment of spirits can be provided (no. 8). Teaching that God leads us through our experiences of consolation, Ignatius warns us while experiencing desolation never to change a decision or course that was determined while in consolation (no. 318).

27. Created by Linda Schultz and Wilkie Au, based on suggestions from Susanne E. Fincher, *Creating Mandalas for Insight, Healing, and Self-Expression* (Boston: Shambala, 1991) and David Richo, *When Love Meets Fear: How to Become Defense-less and Resource-full* (Mahwah, NJ: Paulist Press, 1997).

II. Refining the Acoustics of the Heart

1. Thomas A. Hand, *St. Augustine on Prayer* (Westminster, MD: Newman Press, 1963), 71.

2. Daniel Goleman, *Emotional Intelligence* (New York: Bantam Books, 1995), 8.

3. Ibid., 29. The research of cognitive psychologists "has resulted in models [of decision-making] which outline procedures facilitating 'well made' decisions and those which promote 'faulty' ones. In all these developments cognitive (mental) processes take center stage, while affect or emotions seem to receive attention only when they confound good decision making" (Michael J. O'Sullivan, "Trust Your Feelings, But Use Your Head: Discernment and the Psychology of Decision Making," *Studies in the Spirituality of Jesuits* 22, no. 4 [September 1990]: 16).

4. C. S. Lewis, *Surprised by Joy* (Fort Washington, PA: Harvest Books, 1966), 227–28.

5. James B. Nelson, *Between Two Gardens: Reflections on Sexuality and Religious Experience* (New York: Pilgrim Press, 1983), 10.

6. Joel Kovel, *A Complete Guide to Therapy: From Psychoanalysis to Behavior Modification* (New York: Random House, 1977), 118.

7. James Simkin, "The Introduction of Gestalt," in *The Live Classroom: Innovations Through Confluent Education and Gestalt Therapy*, ed. George Brown with Thomas Yeomans and Liles Grizzard (New York: Viking Press, 1975), 39.

8. Carl Rogers, *On Becoming a Person: A Therapist's View of Psychotherapy* (Boston: Houghton Mifflin, 1961), 22–23.

9. Goleman, *Emotional Intelligence*, 55.

10. Paul Robb, "Conversion as a Human Experience," *Studies in the Spirituality of Jesuits* 14, no. 3 (1982): 11–12.

11. John B. Enright, "An Introduction to Gestalt Techniques," in *Gestalt Therapy Now*, ed. Joen Fagan and Irma Lee Shepherd (New York: Harper and Row, 1970), 119.

12. Ibid.

13. Making a case for a more nuanced understanding of the Ignatian rules of discernment in light of the findings and theories of social and cognitive psychologists, Michael O'Sullivan states, "Given the interaction between cognition and emotion, it becomes evident that a substantial amount of cognitive processing of information occurs in both Ignatius's First and Second Times of Choice (*Sp.Exer.* #175f.). Because of the psychological factors involved in God-attributions, in the first time of choice it seems prudent to slow down and carefully examine the data upon which one has based the conclusion that it is 'God who has so moved and attracted one's will'" ("Trust Your Feelings," 30–31).

14. According to Ignatius, "In souls that are progressing to greater perfection, the action of the good angel is delicate, gentle, delightful. It may be compared to a drop of water penetrating a sponge. The action of the evil spirit upon such souls is violent, noisy, and disturbing. It may be compared to a drop of water falling upon a stone. In souls that are going from bad to worse, the action of the spirits mentioned above is just the reverse." The underlying rationale for Ignatius's interpretation is the principle of "the opposition or similarity of these souls to the different kinds of spirits." The influence of spirits that are similar and compatible to ourselves registers in a quiet and peaceful way because we are "kindred spirits," while the influence of spirits that are dissimilar or contrary to ourselves causes disturbing and noisy commotion in us (no. 335).

15. O'Sullivan notes that "when we identify the second time of election as the 'affective' way and the third time as the 'rational' way, the discussion easily can isolate emotions from thought and thereby fail to recognize how interdependent and interactive they are." Thus, he suggests "that directors need to attend to how counselees' cognitive processes affect their feelings of consolation and desolation" ("Trust Your Feelings," 19). In other words, spiritual directors should not, according to O'Sullivan, concentrate "primarily on just the affectivity," but "would do well to pay ample attention to how people are thinking, processing information, and establishing mental procedures for their decisions" ("Trust Your Feelings," 20).

16. See O'Sullivan for rational models of decision making based on contemporary psychological theory and their relevance to Ignatius' third time of making a choice (ibid., 27–30).

17. Ignatius provides a third scenario that can help a person trying to make a decision with the use of reasoning (no. 187). He suggests that the person imagines himself or herself standing before God on the day of judgment. From this perspective Ignatius invites the person to deliberate about what present choice he or she would most be able to validate at the time of judgment before God. In pastoral practice this Ignatian suggestion is generally avoided because of the concern that it would activate negative images of God as a harsh judge or demanding deity, a distorted image that plagues many. Such an image of God com-

monly engenders a fear that contaminates the discernment process.

18. Michael J. Buckley, "Rules for the Discernment of Spirits," *The Way Supplement* 20 (Autumn 1973): 25–26.

19. William Peters, *The Spiritual Exercises of St. Ignatius: Exposition and Interpretation* (Jersey City, NJ: The Program to Adapt the Spiritual Exercises, 1967), 127.

20. Here it is important to note what O'Sullivan calls "the confirmation bias, also known as the 'positive-test strategy,' [which] "involves searching only for positive evidence. Research has clearly demonstrated that people show a persistent bias that favors gathering information which confirms their beliefs, decisions, and conclusions, rather than challenging or refuting them" ("Trust Your Feelings," 34).

21. John Futrell, "Ignatian Discernment," *Studies in the Spirituality of Jesuits* 2, no. 2 (April 1970): 57.

22. Joseph R. Royce, *The Encapsulated Man: An Interdisciplinary Essay on the Search for Meaning* (Princeton, NJ: D. Van Nostrand Company, 1964), 27.

23. Paul Tillich, "You Are Accepted," in *The Shaking of the Foundations* (New York: Charles Scribner's Sons, 1948), 161–62.

24. Pierre Wolff, *Discernment: The Art of Choosing Well* (Ligouri, MO: Ligouri/Triumph, 2003). Wolff's book is a very clear and helpful guide to integrating reason and affect in a discernment process based on the Ignatian tradition.

25. Baron Friedrich von Hugel, *The Mystical Element of Religion as Studied in Saint Catherine of Genoa and Her Friends*, 2 vols. (London: J. M. Dent & Sons, 1902).

26. Ibid., 1:51.

27. Ibid., 52.

28. Ibid.

29. Ibid., 53.

30. Ibid., 61.

31. Ibid., 54.

32. Ibid., 2:387.

33. Ibid., 287–88.

34. Ibid., 389.

35. Marcus Borg, *The Heart of Christianity: Rediscovering a Life of Faith* (New York: HarperCollins, 2004), 2, 15.

III. Spirit-Led in Many Ways

1. Sandra M. Schneiders, "Theology and Spirituality: Strangers, Partners, or Rivals," *Horizons* 13, no. 2 (1986): 257ff.
2. Nancy Reeves, *I'd Say Yes, God, If I Knew What You Wanted* (Kelowna, British Columbia: Northstone Publishing, 2001), 21.
3. For Tanya's story, see ibid., 59–62.
4. For Adele's story, see ibid., 84–85.
5. For Candace's and Laura's stories, see ibid., 108–11.
6. Ibid., 100.
7. Howard Gardner, *Frames of Mind: The Theory of Multiple Intelligences* (New York: Basic Books, 1983), 278.
8. Martha Graham, quoted in Gardner, *Frames of Mind*, 224.
9. Richard Boleslavsky, quoted in Gardner, *Frames of Mind*, 227.
10. Gardner, *Frames of Mind*, 230–31.
11. Ibid., 10.
12. Eugene T. Gendlin, *Focusing* (New York: Bantam Books, 1981), 32.
13. Ibid., 32–33.
14. Ibid., 34.
15. Vincent F. O'Connell, "Crisis Psychotherapy: Person, Dialogue, and the Organismic Event," in *Gestalt Therapy Now*, ed. Joen Fagan and Irma Lee Shepherd (New York: Harper and Row, 1970), 248.
16. Ibid., 248–49.
17. Antonio Damasio, *Descartes' Error: Emotion, Reason, and the Human Brain* (New York: Avon Books, 1994), 209.
18. Steve Johnson, "Antonio Damasio's Theory of Thinking Faster and Faster: Are the Brain's Emotional Circuits Hardwired for Speed?" *Discovery* (May 2004): 47.
19. Antonio Damasio, *Looking for Spinoza: Joy, Sorrow, and the Feeling Brain* (New York: Harcourt, 2003), 144–45.
20. Ibid.
21. Antonio Damasio, quoted in Johnson, "Antonio Damasio's Theory of Thinking Faster and Faster," 47.
22. Damasio, *Looking for Spinoza*, 148.
23. Ann and Barry Ulanov, *The Healing Imagination: The Meeting of Psyche and Soul* (Einsiedeln, Switzerland: Daimon Verlag, 1999), 3.

24. George Bernard Shaw, *Saint Joan: A Chronicle Play in Six Scenes and an Epilogue* (New York: Viking Penguin, 1924), 58–59.

25. Jean-Paul Sartre, *Being and Nothingi;ness* (New York: Philosophical Library, 1956; London: Methuen and Co. 1957), 435–36.

26. This exercise is adapted from Brian O'Leary, "Discernment and Decision Making," *Review for Religious* (January-February 1992): 61–62.

27. Ernest E. Larkin, "Contemplative Prayer as the Soul of the Apostolate," in *Handbook of Spirituality for Ministers*, vol. 2, ed. Robert J. Wicks (Mahwah, NJ: Paulist Press, 2000), 465–66.

28. Elaine M. Prevallet, SL, "All Dancing Together," *Weavings: A Journal of the Christian Spiritual Life* 19, no. 6 (November-December 2004): 27–28.

29. Pierre Wolff, *Discernment: The Art of Choosing Well* (Liguori, MO: Triumph Books, 1993), 119–20.

30. Evelyn Eaton Whitehead and James D. Whitehead, *Wisdom of the Body: Making Sense of Our Sexuality* (New York: Crossroad, 2001), 137–38.

31. Anthony de Mello, SJ, *One Minute Wisdom* (New York: Doubleday, 1985), 68.

IV. Images of God and Discernment

1. Ann Belford Ulanov, *Picturing God* (Boston: Cowley Publications, 1986), 165.

2. John Westerhoff, *Spiritual Life: The Foundation for Preaching and Teaching* (Louisville, KY: Westminster/John Knox Press, 1994), 4.

3. Arthur W. Combs, "The Perceptual Approach to Good Teaching," in *Humanistic Education Source Handbook*, ed. Donald A. Reed and Sidney B. Simon (Englewood Cliffs, NJ: Prentice-Hall, 1975), 254.

4. Elizabeth A. Johnson, CSJ, "The Incomprehensibility of God and the Image of God Male and Female," in *Women's Spirituality: Resources for Christian Development*, ed. Joann Wolski Conn (Mahwah, NJ: Paulist Press, 1986), 243.

5. Idries Shah, *Tales of the Dervishes* (New York: E. P. Dutton and Co., 1970), 25.

6. Marcus Borg, *The Heart of Christianity: Rediscovering a Life of Faith* (New York: HarperCollins, 2004), 88.

7. Karl Rahner, quoted in *Karl Rahner in Dialogue*, ed. Hubert Biallowons, Harvey Egan, and Paul Imhof (New York: Crossroad, 1986), 196.

8. Raymond Studzinski, OSB, *Spiritual Direction and Midlife Development* (Chicago: Loyola Univ. Press, 1985), 109–10.

9. Ann Belford Ulanov, *Finding Space: Winnicott, God, and Psychic Reality* (Louisville, KY: Westminister/John Knox Press, 2001), 96–97

10. Ibid.

11. William Meissner, "The Psychology of Religious Experience," *Communio* 4 (1977): 53.

12. For a helpful discussion of object relations theory and the idea of God by a Christian theologian, see Leroy T. Howe, *The Image of God: A Theology for Pastoral Care and Counseling* (Nashville, TN: Abingdon Press, 1995), 91–117.

13. Stephen Parker, "Hearing God's Spirit: Impacts of Developmental History on Adult Religious Experience," *Journal of Psychology and Christianity* 18, no. 2 (1999): 157–58.

14. Gerard W. Hughes, *God of Surprises* (Mahwah, NJ: Paulist Press, 1985), 36–37.

15. J. B. Phillips, *Your God Is Too Small* (New York: Macmillan, 1961), 54.

16. Donald McCullough, *The Trivialization of God* (Colorado Springs, CO: Navpress Publishing Group, 1995).

17. Thomas Merton, *Raids on the Unspeakable* (New York: New Directions, 1964), 85–86.

18. Dietrich Bonhoeffer, *Letters and Papers from Prison*, ed. Eberhard Bethge (New York: Macmillan, 1972), 282; and Borg, *The Heart of Christianity*, 66.

19. Brian O'Leary, SJ, "Discernment and Decision-making," *Review for Religious* (January-February 1992): 58.

20. William F. Lynch, *Christ and Prometheus: A New Image of the Secular* (South Bend, IN: Univ. of Notre Dame, 1970), 130.

21. Edith Genet, "Images of God," *Lumen Vitae* 34, no. 1 (1979): 72.

22. O'Leary, "Discernment and Decision-making," 62.

23. Ron DelBene with Herb Montgomery, *The Breath of Life* (Minneapolis: Winston Press, 1981), 8–9.

24. John H. Wright, *A Theology of Christian Prayer* (New York: Pueblo Publishing Company, 1972), 134.

25. Ibid., 134–35.

26. Alice Walker, *The Color Purple* (New York: Washington Square Press, 1982), 176.

27. Genet, "Images of God," 176.

28. Parker J. Palmer, "The Clearness Committee: A Way of Discernment," *Weavings* 9, no. 4 (July-August 1988): 38. Having received help from clearness committees several times when sorting out vocational questions, Palmer summarizes the major steps of the process in describing how the committee works. Those interested in using this method of discernment will find his description helpful.

29. Ibid., 39.

V. Desires and Discernment

1. Anthony de Mello, *One Minute Wisdom* (New York: Doubleday and Company, 1975), 15.

2. Philip Sheldrake, *Befriending Our Desires* (Notre Dame, IN: Ave Maria Press, 1994), 91.

3. See Peter Schineller, "Ignatian Spirituality and Creation-Centered Spirituality," *The Way* 29, no. 1 (January 1989): 46–59.

4. Anthony de Mello, *Wellsprings: A Book of Spiritual Exercises* (Garden City, NY: Doubleday, 1986), 239.

5. Elaine M. Prevallet, SL, "Borne in Courage and Love: Reflections on Letting Go," *Weavings* 12, no. 2 (March-April 1997): 7–8.

6. Pedro Aruppe, SJ, cited in *Company: The World of Jesuits and their Friends* (Spring 1999), 29.

7. Ann and Barry Ulanov, *Primary Speech: A Psychology of Prayer* (Atlanta, GA: John Knox Press, 1982), 20.

8. C. G. Jung, Summer Semester, 1939, Lecture X, June 30, 1939, 166–67.

9. Sheldrake, *Befriending Our Desires*, 14.

10. Caroline Knapp, *Drinking: A Love Story* (New York: Dell Publishing, 1996), 130–31.

11. Margaret Silf, *Inner Compass: An Invitation to Ignatian Spirituality* (Chicago: Loyola Univ. Press, 1999), 75–76.

12. Geneen Roth, *Appetites: On the Search for True Nourishment* (New York: Penguin Books USA, 1996), 72–73.

13. Knapp, *Drinking*, 60.

14. Ibid.

15. Joseph Tetlow, SJ, "The Fundamentum: Creation in the Principle and Foundation," *Studies in the Spirituality of Jesuits* 21, no. 4 (September 1989): 25–26.

16. Denise Levertov, "In Whom We Live and Move and Have Our Being," and "Primary Wonder," in *Sands of the Well* (New York: New Directions, 1996), 107, 129, as quoted in Kathleen Fischer, *Imaging Life after Death: Love That Moves the Sun and Stars* (Mahwah, NJ: Paulist Press, 2004), 10.

17. Tetlow, "The Fundamentum," 7.

18. Ibid., 52.

19. Rainer Maria Rilke, *Letters to a Young Poet* (New York: Norton, 1954), 46–47.

20. Thomas Merton, *Spiritual Direction and Meditation* (Collegeville, MN: Liturgical Press, 1960), 30–33.

21. Ibid., 31.

22. R. D. Laing, "Violence and Love," *Journal of Existentialism* 5 (1965): 417–22.

23. Merton, *Spiritual Direction and Meditation*, 31.

24. E. Edward Kinerk, SJ, "Eliciting Great Desires: Their Place in the Spirituality of the Society of Jesus," *Studies in the Spirituality of Jesuits* 16, no. 5 (November 1984): 2.

25. Merton, *Spiritual Direction and Meditation*, 31

26. Frederick Perls, Ralph Hefferling, and Paul Goodman, *Gestalt Therapy: Excitement and Growth in the Human Personality* (New York: The Julian Press, 1951), 189.

27. Frederick Perls, *The Gestalt Approach and Eye Witness to Therapy* (Ben Lomond, CA: Science and Behavior Books, 1973), 34.

28. Kinerk, "Eliciting Great Desires," 3–4.

29. Ibid., 4.

30. Ibid.

31. Robert Johann, "Wanting What We Want," *America* 117 (November 18, 1967): 614.

32. Thomas Merton, *Thoughts in Solitude* (Garden City, NY: Doubleday, 1968), 81.

33. Adapted from Margaret Silf, *Inner Compass*, 58.

34. Merton, *Spiritual Direction and Meditation*, 33.

VI. Dreams and Discernment

1. Barbara Kantrowitz and Karen Springen, "What Dreams Are Made Of," *Newsweek* (August 9, 2004): 42.

2. C. J. Jung. *Dreams* (New York: Pantheon, 1974), 31.

3. Ibid.

4. Gerard W. Hughes, *God of Surprises* (Mahwah, NJ: Paulist Press, 1985), 8.

5. Jung, *Dreams*, 34.

6. Kathrin Asper, *The Inner Child in Dreams* (Boston: Shambhala Publications, 1992), 14.

7. Ibid., 12.

8. Evelyn Eaton Whitehead and James D. Whitehead, *Seasons of Strength* (Winona, MN: St. Mary's Press, 1995), 23.

9. Jung, *Dreams*, 35.

VII. Embracing Our Personal Path

1. Evelyn Eaton Whitehead and James D. Whitehead, *Seasons of Strength* (Winona, MN: Saint Mary's Press, 1995), 22.

2. Johannes B. Metz, *Poverty of Spirit*, trans. John Drury (New York: Paulist Press, 1968), 6–7.

3. Meister Eckhart, as quoted in Matthew Fox, *Original Blessing: A Primer in Creation Spirituality* (Santa Fe, NM: Bear and Company, 1983), 221.

4. Josef Goldbrunner, *Holiness Is Wholeness and Other Essays* (Notre Dame, IN: Univ. of Notre Dame Press, 1964), 38.

5. Michael J. Buckley, SJ, *The Berkeley Jesuit* 1 (Spring 1970): 74.

6. Anthony de Mello, SJ, *One Minute Wisdom* (Garden City, NY: Doubleday, 1986), 91.

7. Ibid., 67.

8. Lawrence Jaffe, *Liberating the Heart: Spirituality and Jungian Psychology* (Toronto: Inner City Books, 1990), 84.

9. Martin Buber, *The Way of Man according to the Teaching of Hasidism* (Secaucus, NJ: The Citadel Press, 1966), 15.

10. Rainer Maria Rilke, *Letters to a Young Poet* (New York: Norton, 1954), 18–19.

11. Douglas V. Steere, *Gleanings: A Random Harvest* (Nashville, TN: The Upper Room, 1986), 83.

12. Albert Kreinheder, *Body and Soul: The Other Side of Illness* (Toronto: Inner City Books, 1991), 98.

13. Ibid.

14. Victor W. Turner, *The Ritual Process: Structure and Anti-Structure* (Chicago: Aldine Press, 1969).

15. Victor W. Turner, *The Forest of Symbols: Aspects of Ndembu Ritual* (Ithaca, NY: Cornell Univ. Press, 1967), 94.

16. Jan O. Stein and Murray Stein, "Psychotherapy, Initiation, and the Midlife Transition," in *Betwixt and Between: Patterns of Masculine and Feminine Initiation*, ed. Louise Carus Mahdi, Steven Foster, and Meredith Little (La Salle, IL: Open Court, 1987), 298.

17. Richard Rohr, "Days without Answers in a Narrow Space," *The National Catholic Reporter*, February 1, 2000: 15.

18. Ibid.

19. John Dewey, *How We Think: A Restatement of the Relation of Reflective Thinking to the Educative Process* (Boston: Heath, 1933), 16.

20. Anthony de Mello, *The Heart of the Enlightened* (New York: Doubleday, 1989), 159.

21. Lawrence Kushner, *Introduction to Jewish Spirituality*, three-part video series produced for the United States Navy Chaplain Corps, 1997: Professional Development Training Course. Because access to this video is restricted, readers interested in pursuing more of Rabbi Kushner's spiritual insights can consult Lawrence Kushner, *God Was in This Place and I, I Did not Know: Finding Self, Spirituality and Ultimate Meaning* (Woodstock, VT: Jewish Lights Publishing, 1991).

22. David L. Fleming, SJ, *Draw Me into Your Friendship: The Spiritual Exercises (A Literal Translation and a Contemporary Reading* (St. Louis: The Institute of Jesuit Sources, 1996), 257.

23. William Barry, "Toward a Theology of Discernment," *The Way Supplement* (Spring 1989): 136.

24. Michael E. Martinez, "What Is Problem Solving?" *Phi Delta Kappan* (April 1998): 608.

25. Leroy Howe, *Comforting the Fearful: Listening Skills for Caregivers* (Mahwah, NJ: Paulist Press, 2003), 133.

26. John Macmurray, *Persons in Relation* (London: Faber and Faber, 1961), 171, as quoted in William A. Barry, SJ, *Finding God in All Things: A Companion to the Spiritual Exercises of St. Ignatius* (Notre Dame, IN: Ave Maria Press, 1991), 119–20.

27. Rilke, *Letters to a Young Poet*, 34–35.

28. Teilhard de Chardin, SJ, in *Hearts on Fire: Praying with Jesuits*, ed. Michael Harter, SJ (St. Louis: The Institute of Jesuit Sources, 1993), 58.

29. Reuben P. Job, "Claiming Our Inheritance," *Weavings* 18, no. 4 (July-August 2003): 20.

Epilogue: A Matter of Searching and Finding

1. Evelyn Underhill, as cited in *Life as Prayer and Other Writings of Evelyn Underhill* (originally published as *Collected Papers of Evelyn Underhill*), ed. Lucy Menzies (Harrisburg, PA: Morehouse Publishing, 1991), 23.

INDEX

Important note: **Boldfaced numbers** are the **page references** either for **scripture citations,** which are indexed alphabetically by name, then numerically by chapter and verse; or for the specific exercises of the **Spiritual Exercises** of Saint Ignatius, which are indexed numerically.